VINDAUGA: THE SECRET WINDOW

Novels by Michael Ingram

The Busboy
Under Appalachian Skies

ingramcreates.com

THE SECRET WINDOW

By Michael Ingram

Hawkspring Publishing
Corvallis, Oregon

Hawkspring Publishing
Publisher since 2022
Corvallis, OR

Copyright © 2022 by Michael Ingram
All rights reserved. This book, or parts thereof, may not be reproduced in any form without permission.

ISBN 978-1-7360842-4-3 Print Version
ISBN 978-1-7360842-5-0 eBook Version

Library of Congress Control Number: 2022936339

Book Design by Lonnie Mandigo

To my wife, Linda, for her invaluable assistance and
Hawkspring Publishing for bringing these poems to the light of day.

Contents

Introduction ... 1

TRUTH OR ILLUSIONS
Bundle Up the Moment ... 3
Shelf of Life ... 4
Ruminating ... 5
What's in a Name? ... 7
Mirror ... 11

SONG OF THE SELF
The Poet ... 16
The Night Was My Muse ... 18
Prisoner of the Soul ... 21
An Appalachian Voice From the Land of the Dead ... 22
Vindauga - The Secret Window ... 24

BEATRICE AND HER FRIENDS
Beatrice ... 37
Tiresias on Campus ... 42
Box Car Willey ... 44
Benoit the Wrestler ... 50
Aaron ... 52

RECOLLECTIONS OF CHILDHOOD
The Blacksmith ... 56
Buddha Stove ... 59
Songs From the Window ... 62
Pills and Empty Bottles ... 67
Web of Life ... 71
The Seed ... 74
Memories of Middle Island Creek ... 75
The Serpent ... 78
Death at the Stream ... 80
Desert Road ... 84
The Executioner ... 87
Siren Chasers ... 89
The Nest ... 92
The Doe ... 94

SACRED IS THE PROFANE
Cloistered Brides ... 97
Second Coming ... 99
Conception ... 102
Confession ... 103
Blood of the Lamb ... 107
What Is Sin? ... 110
Ode to Virginity ... 112
The Crucifix ... 117
The Will of God ... 121

Tomb of Time 127
The Vision 131
Shadows of Time 135
Flowers of Evil 137
Fossils Don't Lie 140
Jesus Loves Football 143
Jesus on the Sidelines 146
End-Game 149
Agnostic's Creed 153
Fire and shadows 155
Kumba the Native Boy 156

SHADOW OF LOVE
Lost Love 161
Vortex of Love and Death 163
I Will Sleep in Her Soul 164
Lovers' Enigma 169
A Lover's Lamentation 171
Shadows and Light – Lovers Delight 173

DEATH IS NEVER REMISS
Death 175
Gravesites Are Popular Places 179
Summer Dare 181
Each Breath 182
The Deepest Sleep 183
The Party 184
Skin and Bones 186
Bird at the Window 187
Locus Amoenus 190
Another Dawn 193
Death Is Never Remiss 195
Birth 196
An Explosive Affair 197

EVIL IS ORDAINED
I Came With Auschwitz 200
Evil 201
The Towers 203
The Spindle – a True Story 204
Mountain Climbers 206
Prisoner of Shadows 208
Magical Kingdom 214
Paradise Lost 218

VISIONS AND HALLUCINATIONS
Candlelight 223
The Mask 225
Eye of the Kundalini 227
Peyote Vision 228
The Kundalini 230

SPIRIT OF BLOOD
Roster of the Dead 233
Lost Souls 236
Vietnam 238
The Mantel 240
Hollow Dreams 241
Modern Warfare 245
Spirit of Blood 246
Thirteen Second Divide 248
Seed of Destiny 251

THE FINAL WORD
The Epistle 255
When The Lights Go Out 257
The Final Word 258

Introduction

Artists, poets when pressed to paint or write a poem eventually must seek the magic window, the vindauga, that special state of mind that allows them to leave the world behind, to be far from the madding crowd. For the poet, vindauga is a metaphoric and reflective journey where the soul is still, and the inward eye captures a subtle version of reality. It is an Old Norse word for window translated as vind ("wind") + auga ("eye"). This opening, the "eye", lets the world in – the inside is the outside; the outside is the inside, an unimpeded view when it opened, ushering in the birth of another spring; it was also a metaphoric window - a state of mind for poet to see the world anew.

Truth or Illusions

Bundle Up the Moment

Bundle up the moment as best you can
There is an age-old plan for everyman,
When fate greets us with our inevitable deadline -
Even the leaf falls off an autumn vine.
Tumbling off the tree in the fall.
Death comes to us all -
That transitory omen
That's really sovereign -
And resolutely embedded on our transient map
That sets us back.
It's a just a breath away,
Immune to any sway,
Caters not to any illusion or distraction -
Singularly unaffected by any transaction.
It's a motionless sea
a silent whisper - a certainty -
Spoken by eternity
Heard in every man's soul

Shelf of Life

I found upon the shelf of life a piece of bread I could not eat;
Hungry and full of strife, I forced my mouth to chew and chew away the days,
An unhappy feat, to say the least.
I munched and munched,
But, in the end, I could not eat the piece of bread I found upon the shelf of life.

Ruminating

Thoughts disappear quickly like melting snow flakes.
Do they die an easy death?
Do they suffer before their internment?
Some dwindle away for lack of attention,
Wither on the vine, shrink up like an unpicked summer grape,
Sun drenched and overlooked.
Some die of starvation: pregnant with creativity or insight,
Jump on the scene with verve and promise -
Unnourished – lack the sunlight of passion -
Become emaciated - mere skin-and-bones –
Waste away before they can be composed.
Do those that quickly parish for good –
Never given a chance to bloom -
Are lost and forsaken -
Like a seed buried in sunless loam?
Some reincarnate for another day -
Refuse to stray
Or wear away –
A wedding, a death in the family -
A thought burned into a memory.
Some are repeated, when necessary,
To warn us of some impending doom -
Lightning and thunder or a fiery plume.

Some are mere duplicates -
Expedient as opening a gate.
Spring fields planted and picked
Trains arrive on time without a hitch -
How convenient!
Some get stuck in a mental limbo –
They just won't come forward –
A momentary lapse – a momentary slave to the unconscious -
Embarrassing but not uncommon –
A name is forgotten
A date is missed
Didn't make the checklist.
Some thoughts meet a more dire fate
Lines for a poem are lost before they are pledged
Vanished before they are captured on a page -
Buried in a regretful plot.
Some make it after a quick jot

Become caught
In the mind like a net
Become like a cornet
And a poem is set.

What's in a Name?

A name may be a frivolous thing
No rule exists that can proclaim
A man has any particular name -
A hat can rest on any rack.
If a name gains fame from nefarious deeds,
It becomes more than an arbitrary thing.
We do shudder with fear
When Bundy, Ridgeway, or Rader pass by our ear.
These test our mettle with their callous penchant to murder.
Angel, the railway killer, murdered many along the tracks
Men, women any sex
As long as they were available to kill.
His name assured us
He'd be blessed as he attacked –
Sins were something for him to detest
Yet he hopped off trains here and there
To find someone to slay -
Whimsical preferences were his way -
It was convenience that fit the bill -
He just liked to kill.
Dennis Radar was a strangler –
Sought his victims as a prowler -
Bound them up good and tight
Tortured them with methodical delight,
Loved to taunting the police, his favorite endeavor -
Had a knack for describing every kill –
With a placid demeanor that gave him a thrill
Rollins had a choir-boy face –
Went on a killing spree at a furious pace -
Murdering five in a blink of an eye- decapitating one and stabbing the rest.
On his gurney he confessed to putting three more to rest.
Ridgeway slew so many – it took your breath -
Forty-eight was the last count- could easily double that amount.
Once he killed his prey he couldn't stay away -
Couldn't resist another tryst –
Another rendezvous to toy with his corpse.
Young prostitutes were his sport, killed fifty or more he proudly swore:
"Nothing to abhor. Done away with a whore."
"Dime a dozen", he confessed with rancor -
"Mere vermin in the streets that give no receipts."
Now Dahmer ate his victims with delight after they spent the night.

Stuffed their remains in a freezer - what a sight!
Necrophilia was his knack - ate body parts for a snack -
Seventeen to be exact – picked them clean with smacking lips.
Gacy - the "Killer Clown" - buried his victims underground –
His basement was a convenient tomb for those youthful souls.
Thirty-three he put away- young men were his prey.
A catholic man who went to church –
Sat piously on his perch
Did he ever confess those ruthless sins?
Let a priest hear what a demon could spin? -
Dispensed penance and let him kill again?
Alas, the most prolific killer was a lass who could ask:
"Mirror, mirror on the wall who is the worst of them all?"-
Amelia would answer the call –
Murdering four hundred infants in her care -
Adopting them for profit and gain.
Poison was her way of getting her pay -
Bagged them up as debris
And tossed them in the River Thames.
We shudder with fear when we hear Gacy was in our midst.
What horror when know Ridgeway fornicated with a dead whore.
Even worse Dahmer's curse repulses us most -
Feasted on his victim's loins and saved the rest for an evening feast.
What's in a name
That can claim any man?
But when these names are uttered
We question the nature of God and man!

PART II

"What if a Name Makes a Shameful Claim?"
A Name can be like a chain that holds steadfast -
Imprisons like a caste -
And perplexes the mind –
With an enigmatic bind
Where a name brings unclaimed pain
And a future that can't be sustained
Or relinquishes any gain,
And brings shame
To a forlorn heritage.
African were shackled slaves -
Consigned to a master to be a common knave -
Unwillingly brought to this land by another's hand.

Freed at last a question remains:
Why did they retain their wretched master's name? -
Stay willingly attached to their nefarious claim?
Break those chains and find a name where they were begot
Or one that elevates their lot.
Why should Robert Meredith who gained a warrior's fame –
sent the old south a reelin with shame -
retain his slave holder's name? -
He isn't Welsh - why retain the name and celebrate a slave holder's fame?
After the slave holders' claim - amour-propre – he put to shame
Why is Robert Griffin the III so ready to proclaim?
His master's Anglo-Saxon name.
Sooner or later one of those progenitors should feel shame
And find relishing this Welsh name was lame.
Shaq O'Neil is no more Irish than he is Scottish –
Why does he, too, relish in an Irish heritage?
Vanquish this propensity -
Throw off this unsavory remnant of slavery -
Find African names that bring acclaim -
break the shackles they can't sustain.
Meredith had nerves of steel,
Undaunted in the most harrowing ordeal.
Never flinched or cowered in the henchmen's den -
When the roaring crowd wanted lynch him.
"Roblai Dumisani", - "one who causes thunder" could replace his name,
And let his memory burn like an eternal flame.
Robert's not the only one that needs to shed his name –
Others could do the same.
Osundu fits Jesse Owens exclusively -
Found salvation running for his life in Germany.
Thandiwe - "Gift of love" suits Henrietta Lacks -
She's never lax.
Others might name her Ekundayo –
Misfortune and grief turn sorrow into relief and joy.
Hedari would appeal to Shaq O'Neal- he is a man of strength and steel.
For Robert Griffin III, Rutebuka, man of speed, would suit him best;
He doesn't need to make his seed part of his progenitor's greed -
God forbid there is a Robert Griffin IV! – another name from the same seed.
This Anglo family, with its Irish crest,
Enslaved his family and treated them like a pest!
Cast off the ancient master's grip -
Clear the slate of this shameful disgrace -
Toss off those Anglo names, cease this embrace.

What merit is there to live in shame? -
Retaining a wretched master's name?
Why not find an eponym from a great heritage past?
If the lineage is lost - eclipsed by slavery's greedy lot -
Find a name from the land they were begot.

Mirror

A mirror never lies -
Its only vice.
It's unflinchingly steadfast -
Noting just the facts.
A refined gaze,
God would praise –
Imperturbable -
Never deviates from the truth -
Neither churlish or genteel
Neither remorseless or rueful.
A perfectionist through and through
Simple and plain
It has no obligation to explain
A perfect reflection all the same.
Whatever is there leaves nothing to spare -
It is a voyeur and does stare –
Even an unplanned glare -
Uncontrived and never in err
Whether a casual glance or and an affair.
It never castigates,
Condemns anyone for a dereliction.
Casts aspersions or win affection -
Sloppy or neat it will never issue a rejection.
It refuses to commiserate of offer advice

Neither shy or bold, arrogant or petulant
Never condescends or snickers with contempt
Show approval or discontent.
It's always square
Never looks askance or evinces despair,
Issues a sardonic wink or an acrimonious frown -
It never blinks - no one can stare it down.
Never doubt its honesty – it might seem rude
But it can never be sued
For up telling the truth
It doesn't need to improve
It only reflects the viewer's mood
Tirelessly exact whatever's pursued –
Even if it's lewd.
Fearless or undaunted in every way -
Only shows what's on display.

Impeccably honest –
It's the perfect spy
Whatever appears in its translucent eye,
Never goes awry.
It never takes sides
Or intends to cause an outcry -
It only shows what's in the beholder's eye.
It has a mission, for what it's worth,
To duplicate what's on earth –
Not beget hardship or mirth.
Cheaters or liars are fair game for the mirror's shame –
but it's not to blame.
It has no moral conscience to slam.
Like God it creates the world as it is
But never it condemns
Or shames with repentant sins.
If Indiscretions are on display,
The mirror doesn't pay –
It merely shows what's in its eye -
No need to rectify.
It doesn't sigh in disgust or peek with lust,
Wishes to be unjust or descry and make a fuss.
It has no desires or dreams,
Means no harm or intends to alarm.
No aspirations or achievements for charm,
Crusades or parades to join,
A provocateur to avoid,
A blasphemy to behold;
It's a looking glass gallery of what is cloned.
A messenger from overheated sand.

Perfection is its only anomaly -
Ever alert to every scowl or furrowed brow -
Never seeks a compliment for its perfect scroll
Or its faultless eye
That never fails to unify.
It's never known to vilify or disgrace -
That's left up to the viewer's taste.
Breasts of all sizes and shapes
pass by its crystal gaze.
Men fondle their chosen parts with great pride -
It has no preference - they're all he same -
Saggy or perked, flaccid or alert it shows no shame,

Makes no embarrassing claims -
Never stammers or blushes or blinks or grins
Never giggles and points the finger to defame
Or pants with prurient desires for any dame.
Every vice has been reflected upon its eye -
Watched lovers comingle – touch each other with delight
No moral blight over such a sight
Innocent of taking a voyeur's titillating flight
As it peered upon the bed of lust -
Neither culpable of avarice or disgust
Or guilt ridden from fantasies of stardust -
Strictly impartial, even amoral in every case
As it replicates their passionate embrace
Intertwined like lace
Their moans reaching a rapid pace.
It remains unfazed -
Every vice or virtue is no show case
For the mirror to review
For a noble purview or a moral miscue.
Even those it witnessed that went awry -
Rape and murder have failed to disturb its crystal screen.
Even when victims scream -
It shudders not
When a victim is put on the spot.
It's never brags about its successful plot
And declines praise when it steals every act
No warrant can make it testify
Or legal precedent to prosecute.
An innocent bystander of every crime
Protestations aren't worth a dime;
They're useless and take up its time.
Whatever the secrets it discloses
Whatever deeds it imposes
It must be forgiven -
It is not libel for any sinning -
It shows only what is given,
Every vile or gracious deed
That's stamped upon its screen -
Even ones with high esteem -
Are free of any blame.
It has impunity on all that it reveals -
That's its rightful enterprise.
It puts no furtive sheen

To deflect what is seen
Or embellish what it sees.
It will always reliably confess
To every sin that has been assessed -
Nothing more or nothing less.
All the deeds it beholds is up to us to unfold –
Avoid condemnation when it's so bold.
We must choose right from wrong –
Sing our own song.
If we cross its path,
We must accept what comes to pass.
Even darkness isn't a threat –
You won't see it fret -
Moonlight and shadows, it can beget -
Retain any image precisely when its set.
So, beware of its unflinching stare,
Its unmitigated flare to disclose what's fair.

Song of the Self

The Poet

We are pilgrims
of darkness,
seekers of
shadows,
lovers of
dust
where we pick though
dried bones
where the marrow
is stored,
and ferret out what is untoward
in these stark remains.
We whittle at the abstruse
until we render the truth
that mock the obtuse.

We prefer
the obsidian night,
content to remonstrate
with delight
and consummate
with subdued pride
our craft -
a clandestine task
for the iconoclast.

We succumb
to the dark chalice,
risen and sanctified
by the crucible of chance -
spun by thread of Lachesis.
Once lifted -
no retribution solicited,
just the venomous hatred
from the brute fisted;
no visits from the magi
bearing gold, incense or myrrh
just scorn instead
from the saintly set;
no accolades from the plebeians -

Not the least shy
with their halfhearted decry,
and their cruel and shameless supply
of hateful invectives,
from those mindless vigilantes.

Nevertheless,
we sing our song
of bitterness,
rebellion
fearing Armageddon.
We despair in silence,
leave our print
then retreat
to our cave
settling in the darkness
listening to silence
seeking a catharsis
in this everlasting starkness -
tears seep from our eyes
like the blood
oozing from a wound.

The Night Was My Muse

Beyond the midnight window
The moon so bright I broke free of limbo
And squeezed through the open frame
And ventured forth once again
To seek the moon beyond the pane.
I left my childhood room to be born again.
Like a womb it restrained me so
Lacked all verve, spark or glow.
So I ventured in the glistening snow
Or quiet summer nights when a breeze did blow -
Those spring nights when the buds did grow
And autumn when the leaves were golden in the meadow.
every night when the voice would show
It led me through visions that did bestow
If I followed the nightly glow!
They inspirited me to retreat
To caverns replete with the ancient sorcerer's fete,
To dark alcoves where enchanted fairies meet.
I was a fugitive, an exile in darkness,
A lover of darkness and the crepuscular sheen of moonlight.
The stars that glittered above my head were my friend.
I trusted them as my guide more than the ruler and the slide.
They blinked and sparkled their diffuse light overhead
And burned their memories upon the earth for the living and the dead.
Like Persephone I resided in the dark,
Composed songs that were poetic and stark.
I longed for a respite from the day and the sun that exposed my way,
And sought refuge in the crepuscular moonlight, corrupt and divine,
That marked the path of my pilgrimage;
I ordained myself sorcerer of shadows.
Abandoned my heritage for a life of solitude and sorrows,
Befriending imps, harpies and sirens to show my spite-
Seeking their love, so in the day I could hear the coo of the dove,
And the song of the lark;
But found my muse in the dark of the night.
The art of trickery was shared by the imps -
Their magical charms unveiled in a glimpse,
Gave me a delightful and feverish temperament.
A lesser demon, easy to befriend, quite easy to attend,
Willing to share every magical trend.
The harpies were tamed without being defamed;

Deep in the shadows they moaned and complained
Like a distraught lover refusing to surrender to my behests and charm,
Hovering about in threatening swarm
Until I promised them secrecy and fame.
But it was the sirens that benefitted me most;
I unabashedly danced with them in a moonlight spell
To see their beauty unveiled!
They often sat on river's edge, always on a rocky ledge,
And listened to the teaming roar of waves clashing against the shore.
Just passed midnight I heard a harp
Was it Orpheus playing his lyre?
Singing songs so clear
Full of mantic truths so dear -
I had no reason to ask for proof
Taken in by tunes so sweet made me discreet.
He sat on a rocky bluff
At the concourse of two rivers that merged with rippling waves
And made me his slave
And lulled me into a listless sleep as his harp did play.
My lethargy did not last the night;
The crepuscular moonlight and the shadows in the night set my wings in flight
I didn't need the mast to resist her charm, put upon by Circe's alarm;
Instead, a stronger force set me on-
The roar of the mighty Ohio appealed to me more and nudged me free
So I could continue my nightly spree.
It broke my spell of her spell that made me daft.
So I could swim in streams on summer nights,
And sleep under overturned boats to block the autumn sky
When the rains came on high
I walked the dim and florescent lit streets,
Filled with snow that crunched under foot-
Lampposts glowed above my head like ghosts.
I Saw with glee the glorious glow of fireflies,
Swarming and hovering over hot summer fields below the sky,
Blinking and darting hither and thither like little fairies, in a fluster.
The night was my muse all that I encountered
More inspiring than Circe or Hester.
The night is a large shadow that hid my sins and burgeoning tendencies;
They were a secret onto me- these nighttime larcenies;
I stole from the night and robbed each shadow of its treasure -
I could not measure;
It offered me gold that need not glitter or be sold the ounce -
Tabulated on the greedy man's accounts;

It weighed, instead, upon the heart and echoed silently in my soul,
And often left me in a drunken stupor
Until the morning sun rose again at the appointed hour,
And I vanished through the window and secured the screen
To hide the world where I had been
Enrolled again in life's routine,
And waited impatiently for the cursed day to end,
So I could descend through the magic window, once again,
And be reborn in the night's crystal light-
Begin anew a young poet's flight.
Seeking a fresh slate and a new mandate.

Prisoner of the Soul

Prisoner of the soul,
Scribbling enigmatic scripts upon a scroll.
Hostage since birth,
Neither of heaven or earth.
A prisoner without a number,
But free to fly unfettered,
To unlock what inhabits the psyche
And foster the sublime
And on that scroll another paradigm.
Another script from caverns deep
Where the prisoner never sleeps.
His voice is only an echo
Yet it escapes into the meadow
And was heard long ago
From the prisoner in the shadow,
But longs to be heard
But through the ages is deferred.
Some are lured
Pities what the prisoner endured.
It's not enough to insure
The prisoner can escape his cell.
That is where he has to dwell.
Death is his only companion
The prisoner can never abandon.
It's his muse and his perdition.
It's in the darkest shadow
That he beholds -
Prisoner of the soul.

An Appalachian Voice From the Land of the Dead

I died before my time
Like a flower that withered on a vine
I died too soon
Before I had a chance to bloom-
A quick exit to a tomb.
My little place where I rest
Is never blest
Or fussed over when autumn leaves cover my breasts.
The only voices I hear
Are from tombs tended near.
I blush now when fingers point
At my tomb and anoint
Coming quickly to their point -
"That's the mother's grave",
"Who bore the nave,"
"Who shot a hole in his father's face."
Their pointing is correct as far as it goes
But the hand has many fingers not just one.
We loved on rocky bluffs,
The moss, our lair, softened his thrusts.
The seed of life was conceived
Above the dust and soil, the soft bed of death,
A son, a helpless victim of his father's will
Forced to covet the corrupted seed
Not from any weakness of his soul
But from his father's control
Brought on by my death -
They watched me take my last breath!
Saw my breasts heave and sink,
My eyes close,
My body shudder as my spirit left me-
My life was gone quicker than a wink.
He could not endure my demise and turned to drink
And lost his grip with every sip.
Until his anger slipped
And nudged my son to inflict
From a single click
His death from a tortured blast -
His face a bloody recast.
Right or wrong my son became an outcast.

I loved the Appalachian ways.
The songs and myths that passed from voice to voice
Made me rejoice.
In my youth I let the spirits of the woods and dells
Cast their spells.
I never missed the winter winds howling through the canyons
Or ignored soft breezes holding quiet vigils on summer nights.
Now, my nights are dark and lonely in my lowly grave.
I feel the rumble of destruction in the virgin hills,
My casket shacks and my old bones are full of cracks
Like the rocks that are blasted with dynamite caps.
The dust, and stones and boulders roll off the mountain tops
And cover the valleys and streams like a blanket covers a corpse.
Appalachia is disappearing in the dust
And no one but the likes of us is making a fuss.
Greed is the spark that ignites the fuse -
It is the pulse that runs through the cruel veins
To the target where lust and avarice reigns.
It was nature that gave them birth
These mountains that were carved into the earth -
Sculpted with violent care but left for us in tranquility and mirth.
It was left for us - an Appalachian Paradise
With both Bounty and Beauty,
One to love and one to take for comfort's sake
But not too much to ruin the glory of its Beauty
Or take away what is breathtaking to the eye
And bewitching to the ear.
But Paradise has been lost to the profiteer's gloss-
Bewitched to pillage and cover the moss
With the dusty remains of those venerable mountain tops
Until nature's lofty peaks are the rocky rubble on barren tofts.

Vindauga – The Secret Window

We are prisoners of fate -
Nature's will we can't abate.
A Lover's glow grows faint
The heart resigns to a painful constraint.
Wealth comes and goes as the fortune hunter knows.
Infants die at birth swallowed up by the earth -
A tombstone name is their only worth -
Starvation - nature's dearth -
Sent many innocents to their death.
Diseases and war finish the rest.
Between birth and death
A script is written -
A biography for each destiny.

Death fails to rouse a noble plight,
Pontification replaces the flight,
A wretched and lustful delight
in a hopeful forbearance of sin and guilt
that satisfies the weak and contrite.
Rituals and dogma lead many astray -
shadows of destiny
in a web of deceit-
conjured up by the imperious elite,
pompous clerics that eclipse the light
and keep the soul in redemptive retreat.
Stifled by superstition- the obtuse or blind -
become resigned
to a heedless perfunctory design -
an intoxicating stupor -
of foolish ministers
sorcerers of mankind -
who prey upon the unrefined,
trick the unfeigned
corrupt the sublime
and keep nobility begrimed.
The laudable is subdued by ablation -
the untethered soul in fruitful elation
is met with spiteful adulation,
and unctuous behest to seek salvation.

Fools and cowards fail to embrace
nature's brutal and fatal grace,
unwilling to face
God's not in heaven waiting to embrace
I bide my time and wait for the grave-
neither king or slave,
Nor kindred to a knave,
Or a fearless warrior - always brave
Nor pontificated with a conclave -
a nobleman in a pompous rave.

I stayed aloof, avoided life's petty games -
Held steadfast against pecuniary whims
that carried unsuspecting men
too their frivolous ends.
I resigned myself from the pleasures of the hearth -
those gentle moans of conjugal embrace,
an infant's smiling face -
its tearful eyes,
its hearty cries
its mellifluous coos.
The ascetic life of a recluse
suited me best.
I needed no sinful test -
descrying a God, I'd never face,
Propitiating for His divine grace.
I had no need like others
to grip the rosary with tight fisted fingertips
shake the beads with a guilty grip
hang the cross from a collar bound-
let hollow mandates resound,
to show the world I've been found.

I had no need for the braggart's opulent flair
Thin as air - that approving desultory glare.
I had no need to aspire
for all that I could acquire
exceeding far more than is required.
Death gave me a frightful scare -
The horror of the breathless stare,
The grave - an eternal wake -
gave me a tremulous shake,

and brought upon me pause to reflect -
death was not for redemption's sake
nor a bridge to a transcendent place.
Rectitude had no sinful face
no guilt to replace
no importuning for munificent grace
no begging for a key to heaven's gate.
Honor wasn't bartered for a hallowed place -
no deeds to erase
sins that did me a disgrace
a guilt-ridden soul to efface.
Virtue was a most subtle urge sustained
Platonic and self-proclaimed -
derived by will alone -
not by a taunting priest bemoaning my sinful lot,
laying claim to a senseless plot.
There is no sin
salvation or purgatory to claim
dust is what remains.
Desires overrule reason
and those threats of hell -
salvation is a fodder for the fool,
ennui of the soul,
the crucifix is a shadow on the wall
convenient like an old shawl.
Evil is nullified by the fall
A story insipid and dull
A delusion of grandeur to forestall
The Author's shame for the plague
He doesn't claim.

Celibacy and sainthood worked for some -
made them obedient, tranquil and numb -
Flagellation, like a drug, gave penance but made them dumb.
What else but mortification for God's examination -
A tyranny of the soul for a bit of Eden?
Meditation and prayer to overcomes despair
But it matters little what is done,
No matter the merits meted out under the sun,
No matter the little gold stars garnered in this kingdom
Placed in the redeemer's grade book
Doesn't guarantee a celestial nook.
Death is the only scheme

The rest is delusion – a false dream.
There are no pretenses of sin to transcend,
No way to transform earthly dust -
Or fear the devil's paw to avoid disgrace
And lose heavenly grace.
There is no transcendent place
for Eliot or Baudelaire to embrace.
No soul to chase,
No divine snare to grant them grace,
No religious order to critique or debase -
Even votive offerings have no place;
No one escapes time's embrace -
All must fend and perish in Darwin's hand.

Something stirred deep inside-
I let reside-
neither man nor priest could find,
nor I alone did own.
A call of destiny I couldn't resist
That haunted me like a ghost.
There was no deferring
the fountainhead of such a stirring
neither man nor God could appease my plea
or explain this soulful glee.
This holy alliance –
at my request --
I let manifest.
An elated hope I did sustain-
in a wooded covert, I remained,
as I had often in my youth sustained
to hear a lark sing after a summer rain.
A voice emerged I had never heard-
"Open the Vindauga! See the muse" it said
A relentless urge took hold
gripped my soul -
I did as I was told.
An illumination of delight took hold
I couldn't slight
that gave me flight -
transcendence anew -
a calling unique to a few.

Like a transfixed lover near a wishing well
ready to toss a coin to test my spell
I was compelled
to linger and freely stroll
a stately palace
with a shaft of sunlight obliquely cast
across a marble deck – a Golden Mast -
like a celestial flare,
and when the eye did rove
across azure lakes of bubbling foam,
under crystal clouds,
aromatic spices of Myrrh and cinnamon
jolted my spirit highborn
and suffused my senses-
a veritable Proustian prayer
that lifted my spirit from despair.

I was, as if, condemned-
a prisoner of Vindagua's dream -
free to roam
in this sacred dome
that seemed bequeathed to me
with a transcendent eye
to see an endless sky.
I felt, to my delight,
the swirling demiurgic urge
to fashion obliquely
another universe
from fiery tropes of verse
to fertile narratives that parse.
Flames of hell that gave me such a fright -
student slayings on the plains-a brutal sight,
Beatrice a Thorazine saint
with her listless gait,
deprived of her visons
before heaven's gate.
An Appalachian lad
murdered his dad
in their bucolic cabin –
a shotgun blast to the brain
a spectacle to behold
his skull in pieces splattered on the wall

preserved until winter's thaw.
An undertaker's deeds and Godless claim –
cut a womb for the sun to reclaim
the lifeless twins left unclaimed.
All of these I scrawled,
when Vindagua called.

It had no end
to its poetic scheme -
Nostalgic interludes did blend
without end
what evil portends.
Whatever is reflected
in the mirror of time
never lacks a chime.
Viridescent groves in summer fields gave me delight-
free at last as a meadow lark -
I began a heaven's chart
I felt
I had to embark
On Vindagua's far-reaching behests -
I couldn't resist.
The soulful shrill
that broke the fibers of my will.
Moonstruck, as I was, by a translucent glow
cascading across the moss gave me vertigo -
evil deeds forego! -
It uplifted and illuminated
and love was written out of the shadows
into the light
in the boundless undulated waves of retreat
where spiraling passions meet
with a blissful feat.
An Appalachian love healed
two star crossed lover's hearts,
so blissful they'd never part
after a kiss in a summer park.
Another love blazed the stars
when M-1 rifles left scares-
hope was regained in the streets of LA.

Compelled by Vindagua's sway
I couldn't flee or step away

From those summer fields of yesteryear.
Childhood memories of azure skies, sunlight clear,
and rippling streams from winter snows
from rivulets below
conjoined to whisper
to my ear
as they flowed
beneath trees bowed
in reverent abode.
In the valleys
where the lark resided
and the sun benighted
a lively recital in the countryside -
waves rolling ashore on a rising tide,
a morning at sunrise -
the most quiescent time of the day-
held the sun hostage
until the summer sun baked the soil dry as clay
and crickets chirped the night away.
The teeming life that Vindagua possessed -
a veritable tempest -
I couldn't arrest
led me to dazzling heights of ecstasy -
It became fixed within
A nexus to the soul therein -
and conjured up many a poetic whim.
When Vindagua ensnares,
And the eternal is shared
the window is drawn
that uncovers the rising dawn
and the sun braking forth-
a mirage of sorts-
a queer and restless urge takes hold
and I am drawn to behold
Vindagua's secret domain
a novice and much to attain.
I come forth
Like a pilgrim in a virgin forest
My inklings aflame
and no one to blame
for this awakening flame -
a gift from the Gods - I had to explain.

At last, I held the reign
To that domain
more potent
than a stilted religious token
brokered by veniality -
slaves to a tyrannical morality
that hooks the tractable
with pandered banality.
In the night,
in my dreams,
So, it seemed,
in a symbols array
I could convey
the sacred word
of an unknown world-
the Vindauga of light -
a window to the soul
a domain unrestrained
no one could claim
and no one could tame.

Without Vindagua
shadows seize the mind
Illumination is confined
like a curtain at sunrise
casting darkness in a room.
When the shutter of my dreams opened-
not in spring as supposed
but as I proposed-
an obligation was disclosed -
appease the nymphs of inspiring wells,
daughter of Zeus- a Muse who compels! -
and heed Vindagua's spells
and Its wind-eye of destiny,
and compose a cosmic eulogy
of all that dwells
in the impetuous moment.

I was never seen at the window
unless, I was noticed with a pencil in hand
or seen strolling a mossy woodland.
No noise is made when it's opened or closed-
no need to disclose my secret repose.

When I showed them a poem or two, I did swear,
They came to me after I stared
Through the Vindauga
Where the muse burned brightly like a nova.

Seeds germinate here
In this sacred place
Far, far away in this enchanted and hidden space
Where the poet tills this unchartered land
few understand.
Oh Vinduaga! My secret window to the Muse -
Not for those who want to be amused,
But one for mystery
in an that open window
where hallowed seeds do grow
and flowers bloom,
sturdy against those surly plebian winds that frequently blow.
Some bend, some twist, and some lay fallow after a winter snow.
Some are lost in the mist and the haze -
A bit too spry, at first, for the poet to pry,
Fad away and nearly die
before they get fixed in the mind's eye
Like a maiden on an untethered boat
drifting from sight
on a foggy night
a dream that startled the sight
A mysterious specter that delights
That quickly disappears from common sight
Yet quickly construed
By the poet's view
quickly to construed
like an old and tattered memory
that got lost in the mist of time -
a paralysis of mind
a dreary plenary
that demands to be filled.
"Why, why can't I get the gist?"
"Why did I let it disappear before it could exist?"
when words and thoughts give me the slip,
but suddenly emerges naked in the light
that refuses to be eclipsed
casting itself in Vindagua's spell
where the light of the soul dwells,

where what is vaguely known
blooms and flourishes in the gloam,
until its resplendent glow
manifests in the Vindagua.

Lo and behold!
When the visions set the world aglow -
rising from a heated brain
like sparks flaring up from a mighty flame,
Like fireflies swirling about
on hot summer night
down summer lane-
Bucolic visions had their reign,
Robust, even arcane
like Kubla Kahn or Hyperion.

Vindauga's unsettled vortex let me swirl
And twist about with my imperfect laurel
So I could unravel, in the sedgy plain,
What the window will let me explain.
Others have done the same -
Had their way-their Vindauga - to ignite their flame:
The beach is still, ignorant armies still clash and maim.
A loveless world still abounds
as leaves still blow across a field filled with an early snow.
Benzedrine angels and hipsters smoking smack,
Quivering and jolting under the humming and cackling of neon lights-
In Harlem, in San Francisco, in vacant lots-
Dying off like flickering moths
Spitted out like camp fire sparks.

Visions of doom and anguish
are exposed in ashes
and plumbs of mustard gas -
a swirling fog of hydrochloric acid –
sends a bucolic-mists over a tarn -
and into the dell
where no lethal knell
can warn or dispel
before it burns the lungs into a frothy jell.
Ringing, at last, Bethlehem's death knell

the poet squirms and writes of hell
when evil becomes sublime.
Rumbling cannons and bayonets have had their day
Sunlight bodies scattered about in an odd array-
Battles leave no plan for distributing the dead
Just blood-stained fields filled with dread-
It only takes one to settle a score
or make an excuse for war.
The beast of destruction
Slouches toward Bethlehem
whose time has come
when the ends crush the center
and extremes find their way to the fire
holds steadfast to their arsenal of death
No ruthless behest
can put their destructive motives to rest.
Craven fools have disquieting plans
that lead us astray,
and back to the fray,
their treachery plays out before our eyes,
our conscience belied,
our hopes and dreams denied -
who claims to know why?
Who proclaims the one to die? -
An earthly spy or fate's eye?
Either way we can despise.
Owen and Sassoon
loaded their bayonets in fear,
of an M-1 bullet that didn't veer
or mustard gas – the breathless tear -
that didn't clear.
Too many were laid to rest
None to attest
to the glory of war
or stand as heroes to adore
after the obtuse and skewed settled the score
as flowers grew in Hades' garden
where visions of hell do darken
A mother's voice does harken
The ashes in a doleful urn -
Her dreams were gone.
Rats scatter across broken glass
the flowers of evil come to pass

as flames burst in a mortal impasse
and death sweeps across the land.

Vindauga! – Oh! the divine
let me see the where sacred Mandrola is entwined-
Where the seeds are kept and the secrets have slept.
With labor and sweat and the soul has wept,
And stalks of fire are given birth.
Their sparks fly across the universe,
Lighting up the world with verse
Where a naked world is embraced.
Few open the Vindauga and pass through liminal space
And find a haven in Mandrorla's place-
Purified of the crippling offerings of the pious.
The reconfigured world of the Undaunted Flame
Coveted, not by holy robes of the dismissive gestures,
But of the pure spirit -
The Sanctuary of the Vindauga
only the noble can sustain.

The poet is the interloper,
the intruder upon the world
who brings fire and light from the womb of life,
forged from Vindauga's strife.
His seeds grow in dark caverns
On bright deserts and frosty plains
On mountain streams that etched and carved summer ravines
Where ever a vision can be gleaned
Where virgin nymphs sleep and preen
and weeping willows with over-arching vines convene.
Where mighty rivers meander and careen
Through the land- their destinies unforeseen-
Flowing and pressing against their banks with a puissant lean-
clear and pristine.
Vindauga is an open eye
for the poet to be a spy
on the Spiritus Mundi exulted on high.

BEATRICE AND HER FRIENDS

Beatrice

She wanders the lonely street,
quiet and serene,
stoned on Thorazine-
Her earthly ties are bound by man
not by nature or God's hand.
Her visions are subdued
By a plastic cup and a little pink pill.
Deprived of a muse
Or a Divine truce
for posterity's sake,
she wanders the lonely streets,
sedated and effete.

She's my muse- a modern treat.
Her listless ambling, slightly bent
like a water-logged ship about to sink
she's here, she's there, she's everywhere
with her unremarkable stare.
She often sits on a steel-trellised chair,
rusty and bent without any flair-
flecks of dandruff fall from her hair;
her feeble fingers and crooked teeth
stained from coffee, tea and nicotine.

Her shabby appearance bothers some
But she's no bum,
Or a forsaken tagline-
Lost in time.
She's Beatrice on Thorazine,
My favorite heroine,
Mumbling, occasionally, sweet words like a poet on cocaine.
Her staid face is no disgrace:
The tranquilized stare
like faces at a county fair-
hides her despair.
On her chair
She consumes, in a tranquil stare,
a cigarette or two,
inhales deeply and takes in the view.
Her eyes are fixed and tell a fable of pain
Of forgotten memories she can't regain

after years of gazing through a windowpane
On Thorazine.

Her chest expands with a brazen heave-
as streams of smoke gingerly weave
in the air from her oval lips.
Between mechanical sips,
She tosses their flaming remains-
air born-free of her finger-tip stains.
Hot ashes of death
like incendiaries from a trebuchet,
those hot ashes of death land at her feet
and vanish in a heartbeat.

Her trembling hands
and dried spittle on cracked lips can't be missed.
Her lifeless gaze masks a tranquil charade-
a throttled spirit that's been betrayed.
She a Thorazine Saint the state proclaimed.
Her birthright undermined
By a legitimate vice
as she strolls the streets in cold and ice,
Unexcised
By God or man.

Chemical seeds planted in her brain
Brace her soul and make her sane,
sown to alter God's plan.
A forbidden truth unexplained,
aimed to quell disorder and shame-
His way of amusing his flock,
with an irreversible shock-
a pinnacle of divine grace
without a trace
except God's hidden disgrace.
A divine hex
that will always perplex-
Beatrice, a prisoner of hell -
a paranoid thrill-
muzzled by a Thorazine spell.
Her suffering isn't by choice
Rather, a proclamation without a voice-

A victim of a cosmic plan
No one knows where it began
Or why it's a part of God's plan.

A mysterious labyrinth
springs across her lost horizon –
The truth be known
two worlds collide in her mind.
One by birth and unexplained.
One by man that altered nature's plan-
a chemical feast-
that impedes her quest
and deferred her ascension to the Empyrean heights
when she'd take flight
on the river of light
before the Thorazine became a blight.
She saw herself dressed in white
With a veil and crown-
an opium eater's dream-
a bliss hard to resist.
Through a purple haze,
she would see,
the fiery remains
of Joan of Arc.
Ordained, she thought,
To proclaim, in an altered voice, Looking star ward,
"I can save a nation from perdition and shame."
A Passer-by would grin
When he heard her whim and brackish spin-
Who is she to make such a brazen claim?

Visions are never tame
When there's no Thorazine.
She glorified Helen of Troy-
beautiful and capable of any ploy.
Handsome suitors beckoned her hand,
But she, like Helen, thought they were bland.
When a war began in her name
It was her beauty alone
that took the blame,
she proclaimed.
Jealousy, she declared, ignited the flame
and started the malaise

between two men-
"I can't help who I am!"
"Fury and lust ruled the fray" she would say,
with a chuckle and a grin.

Her brain could set aflame
any vision she cared to claim.
Her delusions would dismay
if allowed to be on display,
A brash and brazen expose',
some would say.
In the Bacchic slaughter
She rejoiced without shame
One lover's demise
and the other's reprise.
My Thorazine queen-
spittle on her lips
had visions of the apocalypse
before her chemical retreat
envisioned an angel residing beyond heaven's gate,
living in beatific state.
Her daily ritual-swallowing the little pink pill-
Removed those visions of heaven and hell.
She's not a withered dame
This Thorazine babe
Wandering the listless streets, a worthless hag,
aloof and serene-
stiff like a machine.
Rather her muse is tucked away-
Can't be swayed to put those voices on display-
Neither Joan or Helen are allowed to stray.
virgin or not my Beatrice is betrayed.
My muse can't stand at heavens' gate
Seeing the Golden light.
She sits without spite-
her soul- in absentia-
sips her coffee
with her vacant stare
in the dreamless pose
of a Thorazine Saint:
a cross-bearing soul in limbo?
a bemused visionary?

She'll will gain no fame
From her suffering and pain,
And the script she writes.
The enigma of her gifts-
bestowed as a riddle
behind her ill-begotten life-
is beyond the grasp of man-
Thorazine saint nor an oracle can a plea be made.

I see my Beatrice-
deprived of her visions-
on the streets
in the clinics
in the aimless alleys
with needles stuck in her arm
that causes no alarm.
A manifestation of her charm-
rare as it is-
comes with the hint of a smile
when a vison peeks through her Thorazine haze.

Tiresias on Campus

What does he know? -
Cane in hand, fixed, blank stare like Tiresias
Mounts a bus and exits when the driver yells "Campus!"
A fixture in those academic hallways,
Rocking and blindly gazing in the library.
Students neglect this Tiresias moving in and out of rooms
Never knowing what he presumes –
His thoughts tucked away behind a dark wall –
Hearing it seems an ancient call?
He moves from place to place with a tapping eye,
Unabashed, he stands wherever he pleases,
Scarecrow-thin, leaning like an antenna in a breeze,
Head cocked upward, seeking light -
Eyelids blinking on empty sockets –
Grinding out the days,
A prisoner of darkness tapping his way up and down stairways,
In and out of elevators, through doorways, corridors and parking lots
With an eyeless gait and a swinging stick he probes the world for empty space,
Sound and touch his eyes to bear the objects in his path.
The eyeless stare seeks no friend or lover's hand,
Sees no rainbow over a mountain sky,
Lilting lilacs in a summer storm,
The convoluted path of a hillside stream,
Moonlight on a frozen lake,
Or waves breaking against a jetty.
Instead, he jabs and pokes in a sunless plight
A tenebrous path day or night.
Like a man lost in a cave -
Neither prophet that divines the fate of the unsaved
Or one that predicts Oedipus's end
Or portends his fate.
He's an eyeless man of the midnight sun
Peering endlessly into darkening skies that can't be undone.
Never complaining,
Never intruding -
Only those unsolicited warnings
To redirect him from imminent collisions
A tug on the arm - a quick a diversion -
To steer our campus Tiresias away from harm.
Rarely a kind voice spoke to him
Or tender touch soothed him –

Except for a warning or an alarm.
He tapes and pokes – a sight so grim -
Never seeing moon or sun.
A mumbling caricature,
An eyeless enigma,
Crippled by misfortune
Roaming in a maze of darkness,
A victim of cosmic chicanery.
His fate is what was borne to him
Our fate is what we make of him -
A behest for God's to explain
The secret that lies in this grim enigma.

Box Car Willey

Willey got his name and his much-deserved fame
riding box cars on the B&O train.
He paid no fees and felt no shame,
absconded a corner seat when it came -
his clandestine diligence avoided a scene
as he pulled the latch and leaped in unseen.
They weren't the best -those squeaky seats
designed especially for thrifty dead beats -
a sleeping bag and bed of hay
a mobile loft to pass the day -
soft cushions never came for a rest;
but breathtaking views did come his way, nevertheless.
An open door he could explore in his Appalachian way,
the scenic wonder on display.
the mighty Ohio in all its grace -
there it was face to face-
shimmering as it charged the shoreline -
where a myriad of maple trees intertwine -
swaying in the breezy sunshine.
He felt no remorse for taking his thieving course.
he harmed no one in his pursuit-
never fingered a wallet,
stole anyone's loot,
or filed a frivolous lawsuit;
He was at home when alone;
he knew from his mountain roots
the first-class bunch wouldn't want him as a recruit.
He came and went like a summer breeze – no one in pursuit.
Sold sassafras for those who liked tart tea or root beer.
He took the odd job here and there,
when free from nature's dazzling fanfare.
He wondered on foot over hill and dale;
rode the tracks without fail,
no single habitat did he called his own
any box car or barn with hay for a lair he'd call home
the box car held the most charm
with its splintered floor and sliding door -
unadorned, to say the least, but got him from place to place.

Silent shadows, moonlight and the chatter of crickets were his favorite
    companions;
they never bored him with senseless notions,
bothered him with useless omens
by those portentous prophets
that nettled him with inane gossip –
the banter of common folk.
Tempted him to sin –
the trollop's favorite spin.
Intimidated him with guilt –
the preacher's favorite topic.
Winter's cold fingers on Autumn nights gripped his feet with numbing pain
his companions had no ears so it was useless to complain.
August heat was no better-turned his hut into a roaming inferno.
During the days when sun did shine,
he stole a peak at the divine -
throw open those sliding doors to let the cool air in
and watch again
the turbulent Ohio flow by with its many twisted contours,
and hear again
the ruffled waves smash against the shore -
nature's overture.

Up and down the valley he roamed
following the tracks that carried him home,
no one was there to greet him when he arrived on time,
or scolded him when he was late –
death was Willy's only date.
Time echoed his fate
in the ever-present click of the tracks – a language he could translate.
Willey wasn't a poor man to shame; a beggar to blame.
Appalachia was in his veins,
the gateway to his domain;
its lore, his Eden – nature's flame.
His wild and constant garden
foreordained his harvesting hand
like a farmer in his field
he picked papaya, gathered sassafras and sold it in the streets.
In the summer he danced and sang on Fifth and Vine for his treats.
In July, he was at his best, satisfied every request.
On any lazy afternoon, when the heat was high
and no one was spry,

he strolled about the promenade
munching peanuts and drinking lemonade
he earned singing and dancing on that summer day.
Nickels and dimes were tossed his way,
when he danced his jig and bellowed out his song
hither and thither, all day long.
Summer crowds swelled the streets to hear him sing.
It was then that Willy lets us know he was our kin.
Short, stocky and bald - more like a Russian peasant than Appalachian.
His boots were old and his pant were torn, his sleeves rolled up like a ruffian.
Nevertheless, he charmed our lives and sang his songs,
Shuffled his feet and begged for bags of peanuts to be thrown at his feet.
His toothless gums made them hard to eat –
but the salty taste made it hard to retreat.

So it was, his exhortations were heeded -
they acceded -
to feed him nuts and buy his sassafras tea.
He sang so well, under the summer sky when he made his plea,
The onlookers didn't mind his missing teeth and awkward lisp;
his voice on those summer nights was so mellifluous.
his favorite song - "Little Old Ford" - drew a devoted horde and made him proud.
His lisp-laden song pleased the crowd -
his voice echoed through the town.
"Dat wittle ode Ford just wabbles wight awong, wabbles wight awong"
"Da gas wan out in da big ma-chine"
"But da durn wittle Ford don't need no gasowine."
"Da big wimoozine had ta back down da hill'
"But dat blamed wittle Ford is a goin up still."
His tapping and shuffling feet
were faithful to the rhythm and beat.
Spotting him with that glint in his eye was a treat:
"I seen Willey up the street after his nightly retreat",
one would say in an adoring way.
"No, No, he was in the alley just off Elm", another would say, in blustering dismay.
Another piped in with a note of praise:
"Yesterday, he passed my house whistling a tune;
took me out of my crummy mood"
We knew little about Willey's life;
details or clues were never rife.
He rode the tracks and roamed his favorite viridescent dale
never bothered by rain or hail;
even snow and ice didn't prevail-

a box car would suffice, it never failed as long as it didn't derail.
Never once did he seem distraught
in his tattered coat, cap and handkerchief tied in a knot
around his neck like an ascot.
He sold his sassafras door to door
his summer songs became a folklore.
He slept in barns and box cars with little décor -
No one to bump him to cease his cacophonous snore.
No one to comfort him or shuffle his blankets to keep him warm.
Dark nights were his companion
The sun his only friend,
admirers and onlookers were a dividend -
not to bother or offend.
Kids would ask "It's cold out. Where will poor Willey sleep?"
"We don't know. He belongs to the night and shadows;
He's a crusty old sprite; he'll show in the morning light."
"Does he ever get cold or go hungry", other children would ask?
"He never says. He's an outcast.
"Lives in a boxcar and sells sassafras."
A legend without fame,
never had a friend he'd claim
never had much to say, not even a vilifying curse –
only the wind was most terse.
He had no image to maintain,
No wealth to gain,
No braggart to outgain
Nor was he suitor or a swain,
cared to be urbane
or an inkling to profane.
Not one grudge did he retain.
An unwonted loner he did sustain -
none could grasp how he maintained
this unbridled bane.
As enigmatic as it seemed
Willy didn't descry his fate
accepted his monastic feat
without conceit
or an ambitious refinement
to achieve enlightenment.

He wasn't a man of God
Even a pantheist that slept on sod
and lived by a pond.

A humble peasant of nature
Uninclined to forsake a soul
Not even his own.
Every breath was simple and unadorned.
He knew the forests, even the thorn.
Not one handout did he keep
Only what labor proffered –
singing and shuffling in the streets
when dollar bills and peanuts were tossed at his feet
and what the forest offered -
sassafras tea crossing their lips.

Humility never burdened his soul -
it was his self-effacing goal - an effortless role.
He pressed on in winter and spring summer and fall
Breathing in the days
Forging through the haze,
Red-armed from the sun's glaze,
strolling the summer streets
singing his songs -
even to the Appalachian miscreants -
and selling his sassafras tea at open breezy windows
where a whistling woman did her chores
and sparrows sing on arching boughs.
No one knows those missing hours
No one knows how he got by living under the sky,
how, in the shadows, he did mystify -
appearing and disappearing like the morning mist
until one bitter winter night,
Willey turned up dead in his box car bed,
finally, getting his turn of fame.
A paper calmly conveyed
"Box Car Willey Frozen Dead."
Matters little how he went
it was how his life was spent.
Heads dropped in deference
in the lonely streets of severance,
chagrined by their indifference
to the stealth of his solitary life -
tighter than the knot - a paradigm without strife.
His obituary was sparse – little was noted or sufficed
to exemplify his life:
no war metals or degrees to lament,

no wife or kids survived his demise -
left behind with empty hugs and tearful cries -
no lovers were known to embrace
so a birthright could be traced
and any homily would refrain from chastising him in disgrace.
Put to rest upon the hill
At last! Spared a winter's chill -
missing his box car rides and clinking rails
he rests quietly in an unfamiliar bed,
his tombstone just above his head
said little about his stead -
his name, etched atop, with a caring hand
a blank and a dash –
his birth unknown -
then a date of his death,
that was all that was left.
Memories claim the dust
and the years pass and Willy is no longer a fuss
just his empty summer streets of voiceless songs
and his absent pleas to buy his sassafras tea.

Benoit the Wrestler

Holding high his Byzantine crown, turning slowly in the ring for all to see,
His GI Joe armadillo plaited abdomen, rippling muscles like rocks on a stone wall, riveted joints of steel,
lifts the shiny tinsel, a mesmerized audience roars with ecstasy.
A steroid drama of "stacking sauce" and muscle- needling hormones,
Mythical battles with matchless winners, tipped -off losers, paid well to be humiliated,
Ad hoc champion-referee raising of the arm-rehearsed and groomed before the claim.
A charade of beauty and fixed ends,
A life of rage between the ropes with dripping sweat and hugging bodies,
Twisted arms and bulging eyes,
Body slams, head blows, rib kicking, chair throwing fits galore,
Eye gouging and rope swinging collisions-all orchestrated like a gymnastic class-
Frivolous frolicking, wife kissing at ringside after hoisting his cracker jack crown above his head, Garnered millions.
Fame and fortune disappeared in a wisp,
New tinsel holders stole ringside adulations-
Hard to be just another bully at the dance throttling and slamming bodies on sweat soaked mats,
Prancing about in the ring over supine stunt-men wrestlers.
Fairy tale life of cheap dreams, ropes and turnbuckles, unraveled –
Illusions, like ghosts, haunt a soul.
Possessed by demons, steroid inspired, unleashed, one quiet night, a homicidal debacle of fury and Death,
Nothing less than a nightmare conjured up in the Inferno,
A ritualized execution akin to a pagan sacrifice- cruel, callous, maniacal with unspeakable detachment-
Or a blood thirsty ceremony of redemption or revenge like a page from the Old Testament
Murder was a gateway to heaven for him and his victims,
A dire proclamation of death to anyone who dare forsake him.
Imitating violence lost its charm: really crushing a vocal cord,
Squeezing the throat like a tourniquet until the hyoid bone
Snapped while leering into his wife's lifeless eyes thrilled him more.
The seed of his blood thirsty lust continued into the night:
Pinching the nose and pressing the mouth of his young son with a dispassionate calm,
His little hands helplessly clutching at the arms extinguishing his life,
His face turning bruised blue, hemorrhaging petechia,
Veins rupturing like storm ridden streams overflowing their banks,

Eyes bulging with fear, horror and love-
He extinguished their lives like a priest snuffing out a candle.
Bibles were placed at their feet, trophies of death vindicating his ruthless deed,
Perhaps another ring side ploy without the cheers and adulation, a braggart's touch.
Basement bound, the executioner descended the steps of his opulent haven,
Bought with pressing steel, steroid consumption and makeshift drama;
With undue irony and a last attempt to thread his life with the theatrical one last time,
Wrestled a rope attached to a pulley and a weight machine around his neck and hanged himself,
A bloodless end, neat and tidy,
A sunless pilgrimage swinging on a rope,
A ceremonial feast of steroids and duplicity,
A homicidal spectacle fit for a Greek tragedy-
Not for a noble, but for a steroid fueled wrestle
Living in a tinsel-ridden world of lies and deceit.
His loyal fans still adore him,
The dissipating fantasy of a winner who wore a crown of mockery and shame.

Aaron

Buck LaRue lost his life to buckshot one night -
His son unloaded a shot gun blast one wintry night.
Took out his face in candle light –
there was no one left to incite –
it was overdue – no one had clue.
His brain scattered on the cabin wall
Killed him instantly - left a bloodstained decal after nightfall
After taunting him more than he could bare,
unleashed a 12 - gage shell along with lots of despair.
Too numb to scream he packed his bags and left the scene,
Glad enough the brazen deed was done.
The corpse did lay across the cabin floor;
its head – whatever remained -was propped up against the wall,
one eye was left staring into space -
That's all that a priest could bless.
His father called his bluff -
an old routine to see who was tough.
"Yaw a coward, always been always be - ain't got the nerve to kill though!"
"Go on! Blast away. End your misery."
He yelled again with his taunting glee.
"Go on this time - make it a crime", he said, berating him bitterly
Aaron stood his ground without a frown
His eye upon the little bead
His father's face decreed
time no longer bore its precarious grace-
The exigency didn't pass
A reprieve was not a bet
he pulled both triggers without regret
His shoulder kicked with a menacing threat.
the mirthless blast left nothing to fret;
his father lost the bet.
The "I dare you" routine had finally come to an end.
The deadly sound could not be heard, to remote to be confirmed.
Myriads of pellets did shatter his face;
Some that missed found their place upon the wall-
Pieces of flesh and fragments of bones were part of the haul.
He stood amazed at what he saw through the powdery haze,
Illuminated by the hearthstone blaze.
It could be drawn, from all the gore and the disfigured face -
it was a deed of scorn and but it had its place
years of taunting led to the coup de grace

the remnants of a disfigured face, -
To this day the question of blame still fuels a flame.
Patricide would bring shame
But a kerosene lighted cabin
On the Appalachian plain
Brewed a hate that neither could sustain.
This wasn't classic murder –
A patricide for a crown to be heralded
Or dynasty to be overthrown.
This was a common murder
Of hatred and debauchery –
Nothing gained or nothing lost -
Just a nagging catharsis that had to let loose.
Years of agony no way to dispel
A Tartarus of hate nothing could abate –
A willing trigger and one more spat.
The howling winter winds
Preserved the one- eyed corpse
That lay across cabin floor;
Near an Appalachian Thorpe.
When Spring arrived- the time of birth-
Buds and flowers filled the valleys and hills with mirth -
What had died can bring alarm.
A hiker happened by the Appalachian tomb -
The door half ajar -
The redolent odor of spring near and far-
Vanished without a clue
The miasma of death – nothing else to misconstrue-
But the sordid odor of a corpse lingering in the air
Set the hiker to investigate the affair.
When the blood root, the cutleaf or the mayapple lost its flare
Perhaps it was a deer that collapsed when food was scarce.
A bear perished in the snow before it found its home -
A cruel turn, to say the least, when it had nothing to feast upon.
When the cabin came in sight he had a great fright -
Perhaps it's not an animal's plight
That puts this aroma in the limelight -
Enervates his senses to take flight.
The cabin door -slightly ajar- gave Hades a spar
When he saw the horror of a mutilated corpse upon the floor.
A faceless man with a single eye staring back at him -
It would've rotted he knew
Had another trail had been taken anew

Aaron had disappeared after his untimely plot
Roamed the forest emaciated and distraught,
Until he was caught.
A grot he did dwell some thought
Until he was nabbed - starving and overwrought -
Foraging berries near a summer stream.
He confessed to fratricide –
Went to jail for a time
Until he committed suicide -
Hanged himself with his sheet
After awakening from his sleep.
His cell was like his winter catacomb –
The latter though he could leave and roam-
Forge from nature's plenitude.
The old cabin still resides in every season's grasp,
The stench of death can't last
but the lifeless walls still retain -
blood soaked and stained –
A brutal crime sustained.
A memory interwoven with rumors.
A patricide that some say was justified –
A drunken tyrant's death rarefied.
Others proclaim it was a peccant act of murder
Calling for a punitive turn even though he eliminated a tormentor.
Nevertheless, it must be stressed
that time has not subverted the memory of this brutal death.
But the morning sun is the only one
That visits the graves of an old man and his Appalachian son.

Recollections of Childhood

The Blacksmith

I sat on his knee –
My grandpa Creed –
That was his name -
A blacksmith and man of God
Who didn't spare the rod;
Who with his certain gaze,
Had his site on heaven's gate.
His love and affection came at price
Make no mistake -God's love was at stake -
Occupy the right pulpit
Or condemnation came your way even as a kindred.
Jesus was his man –
The blacksmith of redemption
Forged everyman's destiny and ascension
There was a hitch to his declaration -
Be a sworn congregant to avoid divine rejection.
Jesus wasn't thrilled, least of all enthralled,
If Creed's chapel wasn't selected.
Everything he did he did for Him-
The way he sang every hymn,
The way he cleared your throat,
Maintained an untiring grin,
Praised the Lord over and over again without chagrin-
Certain that Jesus was born again on the twenty fifth
Died again on the twenty first – otherwise a heresy.
Every year, with great cheer, we celebrated these dates with sanctimonious grace.
We feasted on chicken that he had carved into slivers to fit on every plate.
He reeked of Old Spice when he praised Jesus and offered advice.
He was a legend in our little town;
Rang and forged molten steel with every brow sweating pound.
He was the best many did attest- "deserved a black smith's crown".
Forged with his own hand of metal and gemstone.
Despite his hedonistic sweat he remained repentant.
His hammer and anvil were put to the test –
Never failed to press and mold the metal like a man possessed.
The metallic ringing from his heated forge was heard on a far-off mountain crest.
He lived up to his name, "Creed Pearl" the man of flame-
Put steel to shame and preached the gospel with much fanfare and fame.
His door was always open and his hugs were never lame.
But those loving embraces with the occasional kiss on the cheek,
Those winter nights when we sat on his lap during a fireplace chat,

Those summer time picnics when he quoted Biblical lyrics,
Those holiday dinners when he read Scripture
Were all a charade of love and hate impossible to placate-
A secret concealed, a loathing congealed –
A hidden contempt, that couldn't be dispelled
he covertly held hell was our sure-fired destiny
The minute the grim reaper had his way.
We had no chance for heaven no matter our discretion
Or heartfelt confession.
No matter our kindly acts and noble deeds.
Lacking an acquiescence to his kneeling parish
And sharing their chalice,
He saw his flesh and blood condemned -
A pretense of love hidden in his soul
A secret diadem worn – a charade of his love.
His transcendence guaranteed - ours was not.
We were an outcast from his gilded caste-
Ad hoc reprobates from church mandates.
We didn't take communion with his congregation which caused our segregation,
even if our host was celebrated with the same libation.
It mattered little that we worshipped the same God
Devoured the same sterile and fraudulent piece of bread.
Our service was the same we drank the same bogus blood
A pagan ritual of an empty epiphany.
Our thoughts and dreams forever more were blasphemy,
Hell, according to the logic of his flock, was our destiny
He used God's word to defame our name and kept us from heaven's gate-
"To those who believed in His name", he often proclaimed,
"He gave the right to become children of God."
But it wasn't God who gave the nod; it was him who outlawed those children of God-
A spiritual fraud that only he and his followers could laud.
A self-appointed curse he thought God would disperse.
He adorned your flock with all the divine luck- in hell the rest were stuck.
He had, what he thought, was a divine plot that served his lot-
A mandate over the heaven's gate made castaways easy to humiliate.
It was easy to shame other tribes or sects if they were God's defects.
The children of God he so adored were of his lore, nothing more,
And the rest were children of the damned slated for hell that he secretly expelled.
How easy he was lured into this web of deceit.
We were spawned from the lust of his loins- blood of his blood;
From the dust and mud of this earth he gave us birth –
A single womb bound us to this earth.

He hid in the shadow of his soul a secret strife -
A prejudiced bent- and let a flower of evil grow from his discontent.
Each sip from the chalice
Each hymn embellished
Each biblical lesson practiced -
Deemed worthy by John the Baptist -
He let that flower of evil bloom
Took every opportune - grew callous and immune –
With every deed and thought to crucify the lot.
Scripture is full of traps that can make a fool of any man
and have since they began -
Brought to bear they cause despair
Conversely condemn one you hold so dear,
Set you to embrace an overzealous embrace-
Be awed by a personal bliss –
Nourish the of the flower of evil
And trod a path of malignant enmity.
Those caught in the net of redemption
Needing God to mitigate their despair
Caught in the erroneous cry to open heaven's gate
Who used religion to berate
Find everyone flawed -
"For all have sinned and fall short of the glory of God"

Buddha Stove

Old, stoic, stubby-legged pot belly stove,
dusty and faded from nights of burning coal,
stands hot and red- faced on a December night- warming body and soul;
Its Buddha belly crackles and pops from age and heat-
fossils crushed and hibernating in an effete heap,
laminated steel awakened from a deep sleep
to burn obsidian chucks blasted from the earth of pressed peat,
rotten vegetation, discarded animals and years of putrefaction -
unseat it from its lethargic stupefaction
so, the buddha belly can burn this long-lost extraction.
Its protracted sleep makes it hard to spark – its tenacious trademark.
The effort is warranted – It's no diehard -
the heat endures and burns the belly hot!
Lonely and neglected in the summer
it stands in a slumber
idle and waiting to unleash from its summer's cumber.

Buddha had its spot,
fondled rigorously until it became too hot.
Always present for the unfolding plot,
It warmed the skin of the begot
and heard the blasts that freed its lot.
In a meagre cabin near a mining camp
it warmed sleepy heads near a flickering lamp.

The fog so dense
the nights so dark and cold – it spares no expense -
it will stand and guard the flesh,
delight the soul on wintry nights
as it feeds on those antediluvian delights
of putrefacient scrapes
from the burning flames of the earth
and warm the denizens in their hearth
from the bones and flesh of pressed peat.

Its vaunting stare
through its little glass eye -
always alert like a spy -
saw the years pass by
saw the living moan and sigh and the sick die,
while the dead are no longer shy -

the heat they no longer descry.
It saw infants suckling a breast -
life's first test -
rocking in a mothers' arms until it came to rest,
while cross-legged children in their winter socks
heard a bedtime story until they are outfoxed
and angel dust sealed their eyes.
It felt and heard the cacophony of stomping shoes
and fiddle playing on Saturday nights
when moonshine was on their lips.
Was privy to gossip without an ear to hear
or a mouth to cheer;
yet in its stoic way,
bore witness to grieving parents' display
as they stood before a child's casket
before it was turned too ashes.

The one eyed buddha
with its bulging belly and rusty hinged door
was nothing to adore;
its flickering flame had no shame
or cast a shadow of blame
or strived for fame,
unworthy of the name.
Its taciturn way
and bellowing display
can cause a momentary dismay.
Abide it with reverence;
it can downplay any severance
on many a night and set things right
and manifest a mesmerizing delight -
A much-needed rapport on cold night.
It has one fault, occasionally adjured –
a strident command
and a dictating demand:
"I can be like a beast that needs to feast."
"Open my door and let me gorge and have my fete".
"And the room will keep you warm like a womb."

Fleeting generations of many faces
Took their places
As the buddha stood steadfast filled with ashes.
Greeting them one and all,

It waited patiently to be fed and stoked for a heated brawl.
With its tarnished face and silly squat
It burned bright and hot
in that same old spot
in an Appalachian home
with its little dome
night after night,
without intruding or being impolite -
too hot to hug, too ugly to love -
eager to please with its fitful sprees.

Songs From the Window

She whistled and sang her days away
when the windows were open her songs had quite a sway
especially in summer on sunny days.
Roses would bloom with every tune.
The meadow lark would swoon with a descending moon -
Even the red breasted Robin would listen till noon.
She greeted each season from her sweat retreat,
singing her songs with her mellifluous voice and perfect beat.
Even the winter's chill could not deplete
The upbeat melody without the slightest retreat.

Spring themes of romance put us in a trance
Especially when she sang "April Flowers Bring May Flowers."
She subdued the summer heat with "Sealed with a Kiss"-
about a lover who would be missed.
Her doleful rendition of "Autumn Leaves" made us weep,
Misty-eyed we fell asleep;
in our nightly slumber, we unweaved the daily twine
that tied us to her dreams until the peeking rays of sunshine
when the blankets of slumber were tossed aside,
Her spell was recast with her twilight songs
that filled the house, once again at dawn.
When she slept, she rehearsed her daily debut.
The house was her stage, the alarm her cue.
We waited outside her bedroom door
To hear the of her feet shuffle across the floor -
We knew then the show had begun -
And she exited her room like Loretta Young -
Flipping her skirt, tugging at your fluffy hair -
as her favorite actress had always done.
We never grew weary of hearing her sing
Or whistle from winter to spring.
It was a trick when she whistled as she sang
It was a knack that gave her some slack -
To filled in the wordless gaps when her memory lapsed -
She puckered lips and with her perfect pitch and faultless vibrato
Set us aglow when she performed "the High and the Mighty"-
Her favorite tune to whistle sprightly.
To our delight, she was Dinah Shore for a day
And sang "Skylark" in her floating sashay
She wanted to find a lover

And be kissed
In a meadow with a mist.
Take a lonely flight
Listen to music of the night -
All on the wings of the Skylark.
Renditions of "Sentimental Journey", "Taking a Chance"
Made us dance
And whirl about in joyful glee -
We could see she had plenty of esprit.

After partaking of a cigarette or two Dinah resumed
With "Come Rain or Shine" and "Honeysuckle Rose", her favorite tunes.
Another day and another night, Peggy Lee came too light,
Singing and whistling "Stormy Weather" and "It's a Good Day" from morning to
    night-
"Sunny Side" and "Hey Big Spender" were added for our delight.
We danced with her when we had the chance.
Those summer days when school was out
we had lots of time to spin about.
Weekends, too, when homework was done,
She beckoned us to shuffle our feet in fun on the old flaxen rug.
We giggled and laughed,
Became so silly we lost our breath,
collapsed in a heap-dizzy and exhausted from too many pirouettes.
She shooed away our early morning blues with every tune,
And the shadows of loneliness by noon.
Her Summer songs made us strong, especially in June
When she and the skylark could commune.
She was the sun that filled the house with solace and joy.
Broke all spells of sadness and fear meant to annoy
Eased the darkness that frightened our souls
Gave us reasons to celebrate or extol,
instilled courage to against misfortune's agonizing blows.
She let us rant and rave in backyard ecstasy
As she sang through the window zestfully.
She gave us joy and kinship like the sun.

Sometimes she'd hum a song when she cleaned our stinging wounds
Little pricks and bites from the woods
Incurred while she sang from the window.
Promising, after making many fretful dabs with peroxide and cotton,
The hurts and stings would be forgotten.
Once the evening fell

And the pain was quelled
She scrubbed us in an old, claw-foot tub
after our daily rounds with grass and mud.
She whipped and tossed us from side to side with sponge in hand,
And rubbed away our dirt and grime -
The remains of the day like so much flotsam and jetsam -
A loathsome scum that floated about in our sudsy tub -
Went down the drain when she pulled the plug.
The ring it left was like an emblem of our day,
neither Comet or bleach could scare away.
she saved us from our tiny ocean of sail boats and floating dolls,
wrapping us in cotton towels like little shawls
before our lips and fingers turned icy blue
as we shivered and fretted, an unhappy crew,
she rubbed us dry and pinched our cheeks anew
and brought smiles to our bath tub rendezvous.

She knew with few cues
When we were in distress
Tossing a spare blanket or two with quiet finesse
Over us when the winter cold filled the room
with its a chilly gloom.
Applying calamine lotion in a quiet mood
To our jigger bites, bee stings and poison ivy -
the magical ointment that would always suffice
for every woodland sacrifice
she would tell us with an affectionate hubris.
"Part of the healin was in the believin", she coyly reminded us.
Sure enough, the pain would go, vanish before the morning glow,
A restful night we were bequeathed by the magic of that lotion
And most of all her gentle motion.

She told us her womb had been our home,
We were like seeds she nourished in her magical dome -
Nine-month of harvesting before we were on our own.
she took each of us on journeys around the town,
and for the curious eye show her treasure trove -
little pearls patiently growing in her shell.
We were free to rove in her womb
She told us but there wasn't much room.
But If we waited long enough, she'd open her gate,
So we could reluctantly escape.
Before we fled, we slept in her bed.

We could hear her heart murmuring like a mountain stream
Our father's snoring echoed like rolling thunder from a distant cloud.

When her seedlings grew,
We roamed her little room.
We would kick the walls of our dome,
twist and squirm without remorse
Then she opened her little door and let us roam
And hear her sing her songs.
But the last to leave couldn't find the latch and overstayed her time.
The little room was mauled by foreign hands and ripped apart in birth,
no more boarders could remain to be nourished by its veins.
They couldn't fix her little room, and when it was removed
she ceased her songs and pleasant ways.
Alcohol and drugs and TCAs -
Elavil, Vivactil, and Triavil, altered her brain
and numbed her pain.
Silence befell the house and set all of us apart -
her lips too dry to whistle tunes she knew by heart
The years did pass without a song;
The sun was gone; the winters long.
Without rudder or compass
We were on a ship adrift,
Floating in a listless rift -
with bottle and pill, her only gift.
She was strong in her perseverance, outwitting death
They fussed and feuded over her appointed time.
The war raged on for years and years;
We waited for the bitter end with abated tears
When it seemed near, she'd battle back without fear.
just when the battle seemed at an end,
she'd find a way to mend.
She had in strength and spirit on your side
it had perseverance and time on its side.
It seized the moment and rang the final chime.
Not even a whisper was left,
The sotto voce hush of her alcoholic breath
Had vanished long ago
claimed by the invincible shadow of death.
Her memory is a painful reverie on the altar of life.
We hear her songs from the silent her grave
and feel the widening gap of time that marked her death.
And the lovely songs that emanated from her breath,

We feel some comfort when we see her little tomb upon the hill
Even if her whistling is mute and her songs are still.
The earth is now your home - it censors every tune.
The town below hums with cosmopolitan zeal,
While she slept the dreamless sleep,
And we are left to weep
Memories of her singing from the window is all that we can reap.
Her silence is all that we get to keep.

Pills and Empty Bottles

Pills and empty bottles
Lay side by side - a silent silhouette of her lost dreams -
Hidden in a fog of illusionary dead ends
Of uncontrived events
Imbued with long-ago portents
With every sip and tobacco-filled breath she laments.
Her memories were like arrows that riddled her soul
With her every breath reeking of alcohol
And every thought proctored by Prozac and Paxil.
We drift in out of her lost dreams
As the record platter spins,
With a stylus securely lodged between the narrow grooves -
Moaning and cackling in pain -
Etching out a soulful voice with a sad refrain.
Terminating with the "scratch- scratch scratch-scratch" that gravels the brain,
As "Unforgettable", or "Mona Lisa" came to an end,
Then "Malaguena" was repeated time and time again -
A reoccurring melody to transcend her pain.
We dumped her crumbled cigarettes
Stuffed in overfilled ashtrays –
Half bent like dead soldiers.
We watched streams of smoke curl upward in the air
Like long ringlets of a child's hair.
Walls and curtains,
Couches and chairs
Were imbued with years of smoke from those mercurial flares
Held high nervously swirling in the air -
With an alcoholic flair -
Burning between her fingers -   -
Leaving years of stains and calloused blisters -
As ashes were nervously flicked
And fell from the glistering flame
Lilting deftly without aim
And landed silently with those crumbled stubs.
She smiled and blushed and took another puff.

The routine was always the same
And there was no one to blame -
We were caught in a web of despair and shame
Memories bore all the pain
And haunted her soul where they reigned.

It always began after the last bell rang.
Home from school the gleeful chattering stopped
When the door was unlocked
Dread and fear filled our thoughts -
Did she succeed in carrying out her plot?
Driven by an emotional juggernaut
To end her lot?
Would we find her in her ruffled bathrobe?
Unkempt and smelling of tobacco?
Twisted around a lifeless body?
One arm dangling over the bed -
With little bands of suicide scares on her wrist,
Brittle and unkempt finger tips -
Stained yellow from nicotine -
Her lips crudely smeared with lipstick -
A listless smile like a clown,
With those small white capsules filled with valium
Spread carelessly on her bed like small pebbles in a summer stream.
She sat upright on her bed,
Relieved, at last, she wasn't dead.
She lite a cigarette and exhaled
We knew that she had not been dispelled
From our grueling spell.
She smiled and inhaled deeply
And calmly picked a piece of tobacco from her lip,
While a Chesterfield between her fingers didn't slip,
It Weaved it to-and-fro,
As she shifted her misty-eyed head -
Speaking with slurred speech reeking of vodka,
Pleased it was another death-defying drama.

Over and over
Each time a door opened
We feared the time had come
And a scene had been woven,
Her eyes frozen open,
Her carved up arm floating
With another scar on her wrist oozing
Our old cast ironed tub dripping -
Plop
Plop
Plop
Falling in a portentous unison,

As blood swirled around her motionless body –
Like a rubescent montage.
Towels stop the gushing wounds -
A moribund threat abounds.
After that metallic buzz
And that desperate plea
To that perfunctory voice
That we didn't trust
That left us nonplussed,
We pushed and tugged to cease the flood
Anxiously waiting for the sirens to sound -
Loud enough that death would be disavowed.
We wait again
To see if this is the end
The verdict is in
Tomorrow she will awaken and pretend
She has a life to live
And the charade begins anew
In that shadow we wish we never drew -
Better to suffer an unhappy limbo
Than let her be a mortician's bride,
Escorted to a place where she would abide.
We were on time
To prevent a misguided deed of suicide.
Memories were the culprit that tugged the chime -
Brings the razor out every time.
Luck was on our side –
It was only a rehearsal – a mere pantomime.

The kettle whistled the alarm,
Billowing hot misty steam
Reminding us we escaped a bad dream –
She wanted another cigarette and coffee with cream.
We prop her up like a rag doll
And let her know she's been redeemed
One more time.
We shake her: "coffee time" -
Our common refrain.
We steady her shaking hand,
Her head bobs and wanes
As she sips coffee free of a chastising remand.
It's always the same - no reason for blame,
Just raise that cup to your dried cracked lips -

A good long slurp was music to our ears.
Crude and uncouth as it was
Brought tears of joy to our eyes -
She would live!
Just another drunken spree -
Our secret stored for another day
Spared the loose tongues ready to bray.
Easy to tarnish her eclat.
We were the children of the damned.
Pills and empty bottles became the plan -
Mystified by the abyss of her chosen path,
Her life of pathos,
And pain killing remedies.
It was the untold story of a lost identity.
A seed of destruction
That bloomed into self-immolation.
She was persecuted by a pubescent betrayal
Drugs and alcohol appeased those claims
But those pills and bottles couldn't console
The anguish buried in her soul.
Nothing could unwind the pain -
She was beyond any accusation of shame.

Web of Life

I reveled in summer fields
Heedless in my ways
Neither fearing death
Or those daring summer quests -
Dazzling leaps into fast moving creeks
Without a fearful shriek.
Crossing swinging bridges over steep cliffs.
Searched along the riling brook on sunny days
For minnows and trout.
Time and time again
I ran the summer groves in the glen
But not far enough could I roam
From those mellifluous tunes
She whistled through a window
As she kept her eye on her noble warrior
She knew was no woodland stranger.
On hot summer days she sang to the lark and the wren,
Waiting for her yeoman.
When the war ships returned
She held, in turn, her beloved ensign.
They built their little den in the heart of the glen
Where the sun warmed the fields of her husband's kin
And the mighty river, the Ohio, flowed around the glen
And sustained the life of all the valley huntsmen.
The seaman's seed was laid in the den
Her yeoman and his bride multiplied their kin
A son was born and more did come -
All baptized by a priest and fellow churchmen.
He traded his ensign uniform
For a miner's cap and became a simple crewman -
No longer in command
Over turbulent waves.
Now at the mercy of the land
Where wealth was made from a lineman's hand
From a single blast in the woodland.
He bore the earth with shank and steel,
Packed the shafts with dynamite,
Set the blasting caps and leads without regret
And thrust the plunger deep into the detonator box -
Blasting away many rocks.
The hills quivered with shocks

Until black and sooty coal tumbled forth in slabs and stocks.
It warmed the hearth and lit the lights on winter nights,
Fueled the engines on the rail
Satisfied the blacksmith's steadfast gaze
Forging steel for those to appraise.
Black dust mingled in the air –
Settling on mantels, kitchen shelves, and chandeliers,
Lingering on autumn leaves until the winter winds
Covering the snow with long dark streaks like bleak shadows.
As the bitter dust of sweat and soiled snow
Washed into the turbid streams
After those winter storms.

Between those hillside jolts from blasting caps,
Birds sang as hillsides collapsed.
Her songs from the window mingled with zest -
A summer chorus between blasts.
As she sang her songs
Summer streams shaped the stones in river beds
Carved fresh in rivulets on mountain sides -
the water roared night and day
Like a frightful beast from an ancient folklore,
Haunting those broken mountain sides.
Blasts intruded upon her songs and shook the earth beneath her feet
She makes no mind of these fits
Starts and forges on without defeat in nature's kindly fete.
She perennially marveled at her feat
And waited daily for the thump of her Norseman's boot-laced feet.
Her songs were replete
With themes of love,
Like the yearning coo of the morning dove
Interrupted, with a kindly grace,
By the charm of her Norseman's sensuous embrace.
Their nightly feast of sighs and moans weren't displaced
Always followed with gentle caresses and modest blushes.
Once their embraces ceased
And nightly dreams unleashed
They sought their separate ways,
In restful repose and unearthly forays
Filled with twists and turns and convoluted frays -
Until the crest of dawn and the sun's rays
Peaked through the window with that early morning blaze
And the wounded earth waited for the lineman's blasts

As I went my heedless ways
Listening to her songs of yesteryears.

The Seed

The seed did wound
The little womb
Quiet like a tomb
Where life isn't marooned
And breath and time are only assumed
Yet the seed did bloom
As only life, in its mystery, can hewn.
He abandoned her womb
To face Life's wounds -
A child of nature -
From the natal light alone to endure
To beckon the sun
To open the dale so he could hunt
Nature's treasures until he was spent and done
And his dreams were spun
After many of her songs were sung
From the open window with joy and spunk.
He left the viridescent hills
And her mellifluous melodies
Invoked forlorn memories
And how he left her there with her caducous dreams
And how he left her there at the window alone
To reach her solitary crescendos
With nature's buoyant libretto.
The meadow lark heard her from afar
The wolves howled at night to await her morning arrival
The sun and moon - never rivals -
Spun in rhythm with her tunes
Until the earth went silent on those summer afternoons.
She did slowly wilt
Like a flower without sunlight
Under a winter sky.

Memories of Middle Island Creek

An unglaciated birth
The Middle Island meandered the earth;
It surged and twisted and forged its way
Through the mountains and valleys of Appalachia
Until it slipped silently into the mighty Ohio -
Harsh and brutal, it sent many to their graves.
With From its burly oxen shouldered waves,
It can wash a man to the "Big Easy".
Its confluent mate
Was more sedate.
It had no undertow to seal a swimmer's fate,
Or topple a boat from a teeming spate
And leave them scrambling to its sandy shore
To seek a sunny rapport.
From rocky bluffs overlooking the shore
We lowered a lure
Hoping to allure -
When the quivering bobber plunged -
A six-pound bass after it lunged
For a succulent worm
Twisting on a hook
That meant no harm.
With a steady glance,
We shot tin cans along the rugged banks.
Crept in with naked feet with a chilly alarm
And watched minnows scurrying about in a watery storm.
Cooled ourselves on hot summer days,
Dipping in its listless waves
And swing like Tarzan from twisted trellised grape vines
And plunge heedlessly into the warm summer stream -
Feet first with a hardy scream -
Reborn with every plunge,
Baptized by its splashy mist
Suspended in its watery womb adrift.
We skated across its frozen strait
Playing hockey with a stick -
A beer can as a puck,
As a fire burns along the shore -
Its flames soar -
Tossing sizzling embers -
On those never forgotten Decembers.

We plundered it with our joy,
Lost ourselves in our blissful endeavors
Its sandy beach was like a soft tummy,
We pounced on like a clumsy buddy,
Slept on after many of those leaping plunges.
We skinny-dipped in little lagoons
Hidden from view on those summer afternoons.
Our naked bodies, barbaric screams, and youthful forays -
Winsome as they were - like a harmless malaise,
Didn't dismay as some may have thought -
It endured our naked lot
And wasn't prone to blush or make a fuss.
We plundered its banks
For empty beer cans that never sank
And plugged them with our 22s -
Stray bottles floating by caught our eye as well.
We never saw it cringe
Or become unhinged
When a stray bullet lodged in its bank -
A wound it didn't begrudge.
It complied to our dangling hooks and worms
Yielding a bass large or small
And asked nothing in return.
It was a cordial host -
We grew to know,
In our reckless and our awkward way,
It never sneered at our youth cheer
When we swam wherever it warm and clear.
Stole crawfish or minnows to bait a bass
Or a deep-water catfish after a cast.
It afforded shallow spots
For wading tots
Who stole dirt and sand to build little castles,
Along its vulnerable banks,
Yet it didn't opine because they were unkind-
Their screams of joy were an acceptable ploy.
It gladly endured hot fires
Watched use satisfy our desires
As we seared marshmallows and hot dogs
And sang campfire songs.
It endured our unmelodious tunes
And never winces or fumes.

Hobos from the canyons
Were loyal companions -
Like a primitive tribe that roamed its shore
Soaking their sore and callused feet,
While wading along its banks,
Catching bass with a line, hook, worm and stick -
Cheap and easy to fix -
Sleeping under branches and leaves,
Snoring in the night,
Staggering about in the morning light.

It had no choice but accept our plight,
No matter how impolite.
Fickle and moody
With seasonal tantrums;
Yet eager to appease
In a summer breeze,
Or a December freeze
All that courted
Its wayward course.

The Serpent

Old Pete McCoy - a solitary hobo -
Never planned just roamed the land -
Died one night in his sleeping bag.
A quick death so it seemed -
As town folk said -
After they heard he was dead -
"He never knew what hit him."
It struck them as pretty grim
That his blood coursing dreams halted in an instant –
No chance to be a repentant -
No chance for mortal pangs -
When two venom-filled pricks from copperhead fangs
fixed him to a permanent stare;
It too needed the comfort of a warm and snugly lair
It didn't want to share –
For a roaming viper – a sleeping bag would do -
None the wiser for this rendezvous.

Old Hardy was not unnerved by nature's unkind hand
Summer blanched his skin until it turned into a leathery tan.
Winter nibbled at his fingers until they were unfit for any man;
Whatever was served on plate or in hand was mostly bland
Like rot gut wine and a plate of unsavory catfish
Cooked over a bed of rocks – nothing faddish
A free meal straight from creek – "special of the day" -
This is what the creek would yield.
Night had come whatever it would wield
Grabbed his bag and settled in
But the copper head was first –
Curled up for a night's rest found an intruder kicking in his nest
Startled so, retreated to a vacant corner hoped for the best
Perhaps this stranger would settle down and let him rest -
Share and share alike, no need to kill.
But a hard-dried bed makes for a restless night,
Gave the serpent a fright
Tossing and turning to find the best spot
Wasn't much to sell Old Hardy's lot.
Shuffling feet in smelly socks was too much of a shock
And too startling for a copperhead to bear.
So, one quick strike in his lair
Would calm settle this intruder down.

Tranquilized and dead the stranger slept for good,
A worthy bed partner for a snoozing snake –
He certainly won't awake
And startle a sleeping snake.

"Hardy" Pete - his name did bear – had nothing more to embrace,
He had trolled the creek for spotted bass,
Drank sassafras tea without a smirk.
Set lines from shore to shore with baited hooks
With wiggling worms in the swarthy brook
In hopes the night unfolds
With rigorous tugs on all those hooks.
But in the morning, he wouldn't find the sun.
His days of fishing for rod bending bass, fighters to the end,
Or flathead catfish, ugly to behold, eerily primitive –
"Good eatin after a good slam on the head with a hammer
Tossed in pan and fried in butter"-
Came to end with two simple marks on his skin.

Death at the Stream

Another summer day opens with sunlight
That warms the day with delight
Illuminates a sparkling mellifluous stream in sunlight
its glistening stones in motley colored tones -
Green-matted with moss hidden in its shady coves,
Caressed perennially - weather-worn by the flowing stream
That glistens like a dream.
The quiet mummering moans of the creek
Can be heard - ever so meek
Under a tranquil blue sky
By those passing by.
The listless playful wandering of the hours -
Sunlight on the flowers
Dew remaining on the petals
Hidden in the shadows
A fish has its way
With a Jesus bug too long at bay
And swishes by with rhythmic sway.
The harmony of deeds -
Nature's creeds -
Is despoiled by a metallic sound
That disturbs the tranquility of the scene.
A ballistic blast in the naked air
A centerfire shell rips through sunlight
Like a wasp whizzing by a hiker's ear-
A soft death at first - buffeting the wind,
With no telltale signs of injury
Or blood oozing – just vacuous whizzing air –
A threadbare affair
Until the target is square –
Lost dreams in the making -
A bullet claims its victim
A perfect hole in the cranium -
A draggled, once squirming, body, sleeps shoreline,
In a fetal position, head dangling in the stream,
Undulating up and down like a bobber,
Oozing blood in the water
Drifting downstream
Like a long and twisted ribbon -
Red waves unnoticed in a rhythm
Until the rivulet of blood was spotted floating by

By the virgin eye
Of a vine swinging lad
With a grand plan
Lured by the joy of his kinsman.

Their heedless effusion subdued
The vine swings empty – a lost interlude -
Back and forth - a childless rendezvous.
No more plunging in the blood-soaked stream
The pendulum of joy comes to a rest.
Play stops, chattering voices cease,
The vine continues to swing
Until the fateful pendulum comes to a rest –
Evil manifest!

Up steam they go,
A silent endeavor to find the remains of Billy Joe,
Current pulling his death downstream,
Draining the blood from his skull
Bright red like a rose – nothing dull –
In the summer sunlight.
Scurrying along the bank,
Breaking of sticks to forge a path
Like a fortune- hunter of long ago.
Others wade knee high in water, heavy-legged and slow
Looking for death's sideshow.

What do children know of death? - summer nymphs of innocence.
Now they know with Billy Joe,
All curled up on a sandy bank – a scene of woe
Quite dead - with a hole in his head.
Horror struck - they flee,
Scattering hither and thither - absent a plea
Stumbling over rocks and broken branches – a panic-stricken spree -
Leaping over fences, slipping down alleys
Running for dear life- full of trepidation and strife.
Homeward bound seeking sympathy and advice,
Stammering and stuttering: "We seen a dead man at the creek."
"It was Billy Joe with a hole in his head"
"Why was Billy Joe shot dead?"
They all said
Before they were tucked into bed.
These wilderness youths of field and stream were full of dread.

Their youthful dreams
Of nature's bliss
Would make it difficult to reminisce
A kindred soul
Lost to fate
On the bank of a creek
With a fatal wound so bleak -
A "22" slug plucked from his brain
Lay idle in a surgeon's tray.
It was sent as a stray
To kill Billy Joe on a warm sunny day.
Happens from time to time, something went amiss –
Bottle hunting youths
Stalking the stream for targets easily missed -
A Schlitz or Rolling Rock, or an abandoned snub-nosed coke bottle -
Valued targets for a summer creek shooter,
A good aim and their easy to shatter.
Snake hunters enjoy their stints in the woods,
Stopping to take a pot shot or two.
As the shimming beast takes the cue
It scurries away in woodland shrubs - his life sustained.
Backyard shooters from afar can miss their aim,
And a small caliber bullet takes an unfortunate quest
A windless excursion to a hapless conquest.

Who shot Billy Joe?
No one will know -
Stray bullets are always a show -
Many on summer days
When the sun has a pleasant haze.
One slipped through and misbehaved
And hit Billy Joe - more than a glaze!
The shooter felt the jolt
Of an anonymous bullet
Leaving its chamber
For a sinister route that will be remembered.
Summer assassins are numerous -
Hunters of bottles and beer cans stroll the wilderness
Looking for their prey convinced they are a beret.
Ammunition is cheap, guns are plenty
Prized possession of every teenage boy,
Wrapped so lovingly on Christmas eve
A fine way to celebrate the birth of Christ -

A weapon with lethal tryst.
That's what happened to Billy Joe,
not an enemy anyone could bestow.
No one knows who shot him on that sunny day,
The town could walk with a guiltless face
After all it was fate that made the call
Poor Billy Joe answered with a sprawl
In an early grave - no way to forestall.

Desert Road

Go down this desert road
You will not find a rose -
Just a mouth full of sand and dust
And empty thoughts of the Pentecost.
The sand is heavy on your feet,
But your pride will not admit defeat
Nor your heart render disgust -
You're steadfast! –
Never nonplussed about your deceptive thrust.
Even though you eat the tasteless sand and dust,
Enough spittle lets you speak -
You're tongue clacks and sticks
Against your cheek -
As you speak
Of a world so bleak
Unless you wash His feet
And pled your case
To be a born-again and find your place
face to face -
Full of sand and dust and sorely lacking in nuance.

Others, like you, follow the desert road
Looking for the rose
Swallowing the tasteless sand and dust
Following your empty thoughts of the Pentecost
spreading the Word with your spittle,
speaking the glory of the Word to belittle.
They tore His body from the cross
And ate his flesh at a cannibal's feast -
More sand by the hand of priest
Mixing spittle with the host -
A sanguine a priori boast -
The verisimilitude of this alleged piece of toast
Is more sand and dust
With spittle boasted speech
That doesn't cease -
It speaks of love with deceit,
Drooling spittle laced with hate
Fingering those it can berate -
Inveterate and guileless bent
This ceaseless spate of enmity and discontent.

Go down the desert road
And seek the rose;
It seems you never tire
Of dust and sand in the throat
And the endless thirst
That's never quenched -
Spittle soaked and bland -
A self-righteousness wasteland.
Jesus will give you a hand -
Tossed to earth
Magically entombed
In an unconsummated womb!
No egg or sperm
No spasms of pleasure
No contractions to remember -
The earthly measure -
Just one big plop
Of a formed fetus fully stocked -
Popped out and nailed to a cross
Tortured to death
Until there was no breath.
God had his sadistic reason
To kill his son
So, heaven could be bequeathed
Before we are deceased.
He rose from the dead in good stead.
What a feat -
An unconsummated birth - resurrected on earth.
Popped a rock from a cave
And made a heavenly claim
See I'm here don't fear
I came from a sexless womb
Reclaimed my body from a tomb
Disappeared in a cloudy flume
To check up on my heathen fools.
Make sure they follow the rules:
A menstruating woman is unclean
Don't touch her no matter how preen.
Cut off the hand of wife
During a strife
If she touches the other man's genitals during a fight.
Despise fish of the sea
as much as you hate a gay's plea.

Kill every woman intimate with a male –
And every male on a grand scale
Whose been intimate with a female
But lo and behold -
Spare all virgins – keep them for yourselves!
Execute pagan priests
Show no mercy -
There will be no moral controversy –
Burn their bones
Toss those stones -
There will be no scourge against your home.
Defile what you want
God will back you up
Believe in the virgin birth
The stone pushing Man
Who ran off in cloud -
Have faith that menstrual blood is unsafe
Torture is good if done in good faith.
It seems far-fetched -.
Let this illusion have a grip
A dupery that can't slip -
Mesmerizing many fools
That withers a rose
In arid dust and spittle speech
That will never grow.
Up that dirty road
Of sand and dust
Full of Pentecostal lust.

The Executioner

The plunger is set
like a crucifix in sunlight
rigged for the Executioner's grip
to bring down another mountain side
as rocks and loam tumble and glide
shaking the graves of the dead
leaving nothing suitable for an Appalachian hunter.

Secured in his make shift bunker -
The splayed wires on each terminal -
He waits the signal -
A simple whistle -
to thrust the handle
deep into the coiled plunger.
An explosion echoes through the heart of Appalachia.
A thunderous wave shakes the meadows and valleys with ataxia.
Pristine landscapes pulverized,
Mountains decapitated
Prehistoric secrets erased
From those ancient woods displaced -
Agitated blasting caps-seeds of destruction -
Dynamite sticks soaked with nitroglycerin
Wrapped in waxed paper utterly indifferent
Crammed in holes and steadfastly disciplined.
Those mountain side wounds -
Ready for a dissonant caper
When the plunger drops
And wires unlock an unearthly shock
That lops off the head of a mountain top
Like severing the skull cap off a corpse.
Cascading rocks and dust tumble down ravines
Into valleys and pristine creeks
With those mountain peaks
Filling the furrows and rivulets etched by nature's hand
Across those mountain's aging faces that used to blend
Vanishing in a shaking resounding rumble -
Reducing those majestic giants to rubble,
In one ubiquitous moment - a senseless scuttle
Sending bits and pieces of these Imperial monuments
Hurling through space – defaced!
Bulldozers hide the ruthless scene -

A stub is all that can be seen.
Etched and shaped by nature's labor and strain
Mere scraps of wasted land tossed aside for venture's gain
Slick profits made from native land,
A heartless fate for a harvest deed
Banished in dust and greed -
Appalachia lost to cuffed-linked men
In white shirts with a pompous sten.
Why a child asks with dust filled lungs
Was this called "Little Switzerland of America?"

Siren Chasers

Gather up your bikes my lads the siren is a blarin,
scurry about and find them wherever they're a layin -
backyards, alleys, porches, front lawns, wherever they're a gatherin -.
We're off to see the disaster - the handle bars a turnin.
Hurry! Hurry! See who's a hurtin or a dyin –
Follow that siren!
Faster than a regiment - do it all the time -
Especially in summer months when much goes amiss
The sirens will not let us dismiss -
A painful abyss -
Of broken bones, bloody noses, or a drownin or two we couldn't miss.
A knocked-out kid from slidin board slip.
heat strokes – after an overdose of humidity and sunlight bliss.

Each summer we gathered our wits for a bicycle blitz
A pageantry of summer fun – those blarin sirens we couldn't resist.
Just another afternoon tryst
For our gleeful caravan
To follow the "Red Dog" as it slipped by
Blastin the silence out of our ears.
Off we went shiftin our gears
After mountin our metal steeds.
Up the old county road we went,
Steerin our way along the creek lickety-split
Behind the shinny-red behemoth blarin its bighorn -
A shrill to raise Lazarus from the dead - not to mourn only to warn.
Just above the creek it stopped – the still born waves did forewarn
The shifting current was a cairn
When red-helmeted men scurried to the shore.
An under tow snatched a child with a silent vigor
Her father too was lost with his heroic measure.
A weeping woman pointed to the water.
'Help!" "Help!" "They were swept away"
Her picnic apron dabbing tears - the creek had its day.
Submerged too long It was too late
To bring the breathless back to life.
The stream did yield its victims with little strife
Pallid and limp draped together arm in arm
The lads on their bikes were alarmed
Wishing they weren't siren followers this day.
Floating corpses like manikins - no longer the creek's stowaways -

To their dismay the Reverend and his daughter – nature's castaways -
bobbed up and down like floating corks in wretched display.
The stark and ghastly view - imposingly ghoulish –
left those lads shocked and senseless.
Their eyes widened and their jaws dropped
Watching the lifeless and drooping heads
bump against the rescue boat with harmless thumps.
An ambulance idled above the watery grave
Waiting for the lifeless remains.
Its red beacon lights - a rotating semaphore of death-
Flashed across the shimmering water like blood.
Disentangled from their awkward embrace
Retrieved and dragged upon the sandy shore,
Zipped in body bags with a youthful vigor
Whisked away on county cots
To be primped for death.
The weeping wife will never see them take another breath.
An empty home and heartfelt memories are all that's left.
Come on lads gather your wits
Don't stand there gawkin at the dead
Another siren will be a blarin instead.
Hop up on your handle-bar steed -
It's ready-made a heavy metal breed.
Won't buck - a little oil is all it needs.
So, mount and ride my lads -
Make plans –
The reverend and his daughter met God's demands –
A good drowning at his divine Hand
Fills the churches with adulations and commands –
Warms the tongue with rumors and small talk.
Just another summer day at the creek.
Swimmers invade it with joyful shrieks
Swat and kick at it with fists and feet –
Rivalries at different turgid feats.
Boaters hack it up with blades or beat it with oars -
Fishermen lash it, whip and poke it,
Even tickle it with drooping rods and whirling strings -
Those fun-loving never quit
Painters expose it, parade it in art galleries and living rooms –
Those impudent braggarts!
Once in while someone dies in it –
God's regretful smile?
Rumbling and swirling it takes its revenge,

Even a minister and the rose of his life - his pink cheeked daughter -
flush from the summer sun.
Hop up on those steeds
Follow that lusty seductress before the autumn leaves!
Ride away - find more joyful deeds
The summer is young –
The song of the sirens is filled with titillating leads.

The Nest

The cabin's musty smell and dusty shelves fouls the air
Sneezing bouts are a common affair
When the door opens to a dusty fanfare.
Time to clean the house from stem to stern -
Purge the dust from sleepy shelves,
Cobwebs from lonely corners,
Clumps of dripped honey - molasses too - from sticky cupboards,
Grease and stains from oven walls -
And grime on the family diary of meals past.
Each of us ply our craft –
A coup de grace on muck and dust until we bust -
Sweeping and swabbing floors with bleeding blisters
Scrubbing countertops stained with ketchup and mustard
Dusting shelves with lemon-oiled dusters.
Dirty and spent
One chore remains we can't circumvent
A dresser drawer we'd like to exempt –
"Get the TNT or we'll be here until dawn",
A young one recommends.
Lifting our spirits before the cleaning begins.
Dusting comes first and the drawers are next -
Behold! A nest was formed
Shredded cloth and napkins torn
Razor sharp teeth and dainty claws forged this little prideful den
Crafted well - a mother's touch - neat and clean
Molded from nature's scheme -
As good as any engineer could dream.
Little peeps of scorn foretold -
Little mice - a week or two old,
Plummeting to the floor
And scurried out the door
Like unwanted visitors
Tumbling and rolling across the yard.
The nest dispersed
Like a windy cloudburst
Its swaddling paper and cloth interspersed
As the swaddling debris was tossed among the leaves and grass -
A tumbling mess.
Their hope for tender care in their secluded nest
Was transposed into the open air unpossessed.
The mother scurried about gathering them up

Their little beds and tattered sheets
Are lost to a summer breeze.
Her efforts are in vain
The brood is fair game
For circling birds to claim
And pluck the youthful prey quickly slain.
Swooping down with open talons
Seeking their early morning rations
That nature sanctions
Shortly after they left their mother's womb.
Their heads are clamped and crushed - ready to be consumed.
One sweep is all it took –
Their flight is booked –
Wiggling morsels in the air
A feast in a snare,
A struggling hors d'oeuvre.
Fruitless to fetch food for the day,
Her nest destroyed - a well- hidden lair;
Feast only for her share –
Her progeny ensnared.
No need to tend to their welfare
And snacks upon what nature declares –
Another mother's brood.

The Doe

A little doe met my eyes
Shortly after sunrise.
Its head cocked and upright
Perched on a long slender neck.
Its large oval eyes, so alert and coy,
Cast a subtle ploy -
To disguise its distress -
Tricked me to think it was merely taking a rest,
Since it didn't flee
When it spotted me.
I presumed it was unafraid -
Didn't think of me as a foe
I was convinced it liked me so.
Little did I know
Its fixed stare
Was one of despair -
I didn't share.
I thought, for reasons I couldn't explain,
Her wildness had been tamed,
Or I had gained saintly fame
That God had suddenly ordained.
No matter the scheme proclaimed
I thought it was my friend -
It never once dismissed me
And charged away in frightened spree.
The attention gave me hope
So, I spoke
Cautiously in soft tones.
I thought she'd found a home -
my good fortune as it reposed.
So I turned away to brag of my good fortune
And called to my wife – an earnest importune -
"Come here my dear and see the little deer",
I said to her with good cheer.
Presuming it was sitting quietly and still alive
I Resumed with a prideful glance
To resume our heralded trance.
Its eyes were still open and wide
And starring at the sky.
Its head and neck had drifted backwards,
Bent and resting on the ground.

"Never mind" I said to my wife
With consternation and strife
"I guess she never found her home."
"At least a place where she can roam."
Now I knew it wasn't my friend
Or was a saint to be that I could defend.
My wife could plainly see the poor doe was dead.
And why its poor mother wasn't at its side -
She had abandoned it
And didn't want to see the dread
Of her the blood-soaked babe
Curled up in the shade
On that bright summer day.

Sacred Is the Profane

Cloistered Brides

A Carmelite nun enters young,
sacrifices life for monastic tongue.
Forbidden the fruits of a loving affair -
always in despair – this loving pair
on her knees beckoning with a whispering prayer,
hope that Jesus will step forward
and be honored
and grant her a loving fanfare
and replace her sensuous need
for a stifling creed
and strip away her freedom for a plat
except to sleep on a hardened slat
and kneel on hardened knees -
a rag in hand to squeeze -
to scrub floors of stone or slate.
Her masochistic retreat titillates –
accolades for her heavenly fate
a tearful apocalyptic penance -
to be a saintly tenant
endless pressing beads,
as a rosary swings about her knees.
bowing and genuflecting in dingy robes
with a deep gasp
her beseeching hands clasped
pleads her case -
nothing lewd or perverse,
Just those blood-soaked shorts -
the curse –
my unseeded report,
To gain God's support.

A heavenly largesse is at stake,
vows of chastity insure the prize -an eternal keepsake.
Unconsummated embrace is decreed,
fleshly love forestalled by creed -
but a distant lover far and wide
shared appropriately with every bride;
No jealousy when He arrives,
naked and strapped to cross -
all bow in mutual reverence -
multiple marriages are allowed! -

Spiritual polygamy - a holy harem even avowed,
a divine alliance is espoused -
quite a fete for a Husband –
He doesn't have to pick
He's won their hearts – it's very slick
He has them all
in one divine free for all.

They come with open arms - habitat and all – to a divine picnic -
a celibate Woodstock
with vestal virgins supplicating to their joyful chastity -
undefiled and devoted -
a perfect Man who can do no wrong –
easy to thwart those passionate caress
resist those sensual embraces -
the hymen intact -
just the seed of blood to extract
the womb to contract,
as those blood drenched rags
are tossed in bags
and kept out of sight.
He's the right Man for a joyful knell;
He's worth a dismal puritanical cell
with a simple lair of straw
never to suffer a carnal faux pas
or an avarice spell.

A candle lights their dismal path,
back to their cell to uphold their celibate oath
and subdue their regret
and await the dreams that might be left.
But obeisance smoothers dreams,
stifles love and fantasies.

Second Coming

When Jesus returns,
He can celebrate a spiritus mundi
Of black blood drained from the earth,
And the glee and mirth
Of heedless consumption -
SUV moms, - metal weapons to kill and not to be killed –
"Your children not mine!" she can disclaim
After the collision and flames.
"Better yours than mine!"
"Spare my bloodline" -
"Cart their corpses away"
"Too bad if they had a baby"
"Get a Himi or a Yukon XL!"
"Save your baby from a crushed skull" -
"No need for a bloody repartee."
"I don't mean to be facetious."
"Stick around and be with Jesus."
"Be a prig"
"Protect your offspring!" -
"Get a gas guzzling rig."
"That's my advice –
"Be here for the Second Advent"
"See our SUVs sitting in Sunday morning parking lots."
"See how we pollute"
"See our children coughing up soot";
"They understood" -
"They'll see our devoted greed afoot."
"For Jesus's sake"
"We care not what's at stake"
"As long as our tanks are full"
"And our SUVs have plenty of pull" -
"Capable of wiping out those thoughtless fools."

IF the Hemi or the XL are mediocre
Become a born-again Expedition owner.
It's such a temptation
For any Christian -
It guarantees an invitation
To the Lord's second resurrection.
It might make Jesus choke a bit
But He'll see the evangelical spirit -

Protect your own;
The Second Coming is sown.

God loves the Ford 350
Lots of room and pulling power -
Satisfy His religious scheme -
Chug His Son to Calvary to be redeemed.
Enliven His dream –
Especially if it had four-wheel drive
That guzzles and chimes.

The Armada and the Sequoia are top of the line -
Don't pollute much on a dime –
But feed them a dollar and more time –
Jesus will choke on the smoke and grime.
Nothing like being redeemed
In polluted air and slime.

That's all that counts
With God's fruitful plan
When the Second Coming is at hand -
And those flame tipped wands
Keep burning on the land
And pump jacks gleefully nod up and down
Emptying the ground of the obsidian gold
To lube those cylinder walls
So those pistons can slide without any flaws -
Combusting in those silent chambers
Spewing out carbon trails without a disclaimer
Into the naked air to please our Savior.

This was inspired after His first visit to Calvary.
He'd be pleased at the joyful reunion
To inhale the fetid air from all the pollution
And cruise around in a Silverado or a Tundra
And bear witness to all the suffering, torture, and executions,
That kicked off the faith
Before the Second Coming
And kept it humming
While myriads of children were starving
Dying of diseases fatal and undeserving.
Hear those fervent sermons
When plagues caused so much death and aversion.

He'd see the religions fighting and feuding -
And the scathing struggle to see which one needed excluding.
Each had heaven - sight unseen
And claimed the same doctrine holy and clean
Yet insisted only one had the proper scheme.
Then slaughtered each other for that rightful claim.
He'd see with a delight glee
We've transcended this frightful killing
And only massacre and pollute with our SUVs.

And, certainly, believe Jesus would side with them
And find ways to fault and condemn
Their self-righteous kin
He must declare the rest pretend.

Conception

Consummation bears the seed of despair;
It struggles to cease its tender snare
and seeks to flee the womb,
after it blooms,
and prowl in the sun of extinction.
Death lingers in germination.
The dark night of the womb,
welcomed one lowly visitor - entombed.
After the seductive and blissful storm
it taps at the restricted door
seeking its lowly alcove –
where it holds its own – a silent standoff.
A simple, subterranean spark
hiding in the dark
a stowaway in the blood coursing womb -
a sanctuary and a sepulcher -
thrust, at last, into the stormy sea of life -
an imperative heist -
cast into the ebb and flow of joy and despair, love and hate,
into the relentless grip of time and fate.
Some have a brief pilgrimage,
linger at the gate
long overdue until it's too late
and can't escape –
seized at last without a breath.
Others twist and turn in wait
thrust through the gate
but is met with an early fate.
Some are hard worn, and make it late
And perish in their sleep.
Diseases and accidents find many others
and take them without their druthers.
There is only one chance to make the dance -
it's a dictum without a nuance -
death takes your hand and leads the way
no one knows how long you'll stay.

Confession

He preserves his soul for another day
As he settles in the confessional booth to pray.
He whispers his sins through that darkened window
As many penitents have, before him, spoken through the trellised portal.
The priest approves the stale news
The penitent is free of being traduced.
As he utters his penance on his knees,
A mirthful chuckle gave hints of glee
When his sins were set free.
He starts anew
A fresh vow to fight his baleful thoughts
That plagued him with the same tempting plots.
He resists with all his might,
But soon falls into his sinful plight.
A curse word falls from his lips
Or a vilifying blue streak when it fits,
Sometimes, now and again, with pummeling fists.
These are prideful and easy to confess.
But there is the one he can never resist -
Culpable and resolute as he knows it is -
He's too embarrassed to let it fall from his lips
But guilt tilts the mind to luminesce
Those nightly caresses,
So, he pleads his woeful case –
A revolving door of disgrace.
"Be good my son" the priest behests
After he's confessed,
But knows he will soon be vexed
And return by Sunday next.

Communion promises him a place
Beyond heaven's gate
If he can resist his sinful fate
And retain equal shares in God's grace.
The priest's Pentecostal touch
Will save him from any sinful clutch
And the portal doors will open wide,
And he'll be safe if he died -
A denizen of heaven
With Jesus on his side -
His Father, too, with His monistic pride.

Confession is the guide
To free the soul to eat that tasteless host
And earn the love of the Holy Ghost.

His confessor is there to judge,
Grant redemption without a grudge,
To get the penitent to avoid a sinful trudge.
A Hail Mary and an Act of Contrition will suffice
To save his soul from vice.
He's a shoe-in for paradise -
A divine prize for a worthy priest –
God's errand boy -
Who did His bidding and made his ploy,
To coerce the penitent to feel contrite
And opt for grace
And beckons the sinner to seek God's heavenly place
And repeat the dreary mantra -
For redemption's sake -
"Bless me father for I have sinned"
While kneeling in a wooden stall
Seeking atonement
Against the impending omen;
His heart seduced
His soul beguiled
To disclose his intimate secret
To a furtive curate's
Intimidating way to coax
The rueful penitent that God's not a hoax
And sin can't be revoked
Unless the veil is lifted
And God's emissary is scripted.
The array of sins must be explained
So, the sinner can be saved.
The venial sins of cursing and fibbing are first in line -
Heaven won't be declined.
Mortal sin is too embarrassing to define.
The sin of lust can't be discussed -
Causes too much disgust
And God's mistrust.
Under the sheets
It's quite a treat
But telling it to the priest
Must be tiring to the extreme

And the unrelenting chime –
"How many times my boy?", the ghostly priest will ask
Hidden behind the trellised cage –
The mockery that is staged
For God to witness in His hermitage.
Let me count the ways, the lad thinks;
My penance will redeem my jinx
So, give him the number of times
So, I can justify my crime.

The timid boy recoils
With contrite remorse prevails
And confesses to the sum
Give or take a few -
The tally skewed
By the penitent's claim -
And mumbles through cage to abate the shame.
"Abusing your self is a horrible offence", the priest proclaims
"It's obscene and profane"
"God can't save you from Satan's flames" -
His homily unconstrained.
His penance served;
Absolution observed
Waving his hand like a magic wand, blessing him in the dark.
"Three "Hail Marys" and "four "Our Fathers", the priest would say,
The state of grace ordained –
Contrite again for another day.

He leaves the church on a summer eve,
Granted, once again, another reprieve.
Purged of sin and the scent of incense on his skin,
The chatter of delight emanating in the night
Tempts him once again
To repeat the sin.
Gathered in the street light glow -
A luminous hallo -
Smiling maidens in a row
Beckon him to make a vow in his afterglow.
A glance, a smile, and a wink,
Redemption fades and grows indistinct -
Perfume rouses his temptation
Rendering no cessation
The time has come to pluck the plumb

And vanquish the holy scent
Of that unctuous incense.
He appraises them with another glance;
He'll sin for a chance;
He'll be forgiven for a little romance -
A little delight in the heat of the night.
No need to check those passionate caresses that excite -
He can become contrite once again
When the priest absolves him of his sin.

Blood of the Lamb

Religion is a harlot that seduces the mind
Makes cuckolds of the best as it maligns.
Ready to condemn or cast the first stone -
Makes no difference if they writhe in pain or groan
They must atone!
They must atone!
Redemption is the spool
And guilt is the thread that twists the fool
In the vestibule
To cast those stones
And hear the dissenter's groans.
Love is not far from their lips
As long as self-righteous creeds mark their eclipse
And sanctifies their self-righteous interdict,
And their bloody ascension after the apocalypse.
There is no shame in purging the land
As long as Jesus's blood is sustained
And another crusade can save mankind
From dissenters who won't repent
From malcontents who refuse to relent.
There is no shame in going amok
Let the blood ooze like a flood
In the clefts of dirt and mud
Leave the sinner's corpses for vultures and bugs.
Redemption is the creed
For their war mongering deeds.
In the name of the Father and the Son and the Holy Ghost -
Consume the host
Take those dissenters and hang them on bloody posts.
Liberate them for the Pentecost
If not, God smiles from his abode -
Left to dote when more are smote.
Those killing fields of yesteryear -
Massacres of despair
In unremorseful tombs still echo with a silent cheer
Where those heathens are buried
With God's acceded hand
And his Mercenaries' demands -
His warriors with their sanctimonious behests
Who continue His campaign and never digress.
To drain blood of death for many a sepulcher.

Massacred in droves to be the rightful heirs?
The Pope in Rome and God in Heaven the cross to bear?
Those who refused obeisance to either two did despair after the accord
Were sliced in parts by many a kindly Christian sword
Stacked like cairn At St. Lambert's church to scorn- a pagan's feast to behold!
To mend the wounds of bloody treachery and further religious zealotry
A wedding and massacre were set to celebrate an apostle's day,
Who saw Christ's ascension and could not stray!
Yet hatred sparked the resolute and tyrannical foray.
That beckons to the conscience that even God can't repay.
And questions persist to this day.
Which side did God want slaughtered in the zealot's fray?
Did heavens weep or celebrate at the Calvinist's massacre?
Or praise and dance at the best Catholic executor?
Did a divine wand touch the souls of those who slaughtered the most?
Fought the hardest to perpetrate the bloody Pentecost?
Which did God appreciate the most -
Anabaptists' bleeding body parts decomposing in cages
The Huguenots' corpses floating in the Seine
Or putrefying in the streets after the Parisian purge?
Perhaps Satan is to blame
The scape goat for every vile act of shame
Coaxed these persecutors of Christ to rend and slice for fame
But God can sort through those acts of vicious acclaim
Heaven is secured for those who massacred without intention to inflame
The Redeemer's mercy is a fleabane
That determines the noble slayers from ignoble ones.
The merciful executioners from the cruel puissant ones.
Exterminate, humiliate the inhuman beasts- the Huguenots are to blame
Let the carrions devour the corpses of the slain.
Let the Seine wash them away and leave no stain-
Baptism of the dead - His will be sustained.
Militant sermons sanctioned by God will redeem any deed.
For the Redeemer's sake heresy has to be restrained
Torture, maim fight to gain a monopoly on hate.
As long as it's won with a purity of heart.
Does God take mercy on this murderous rage
As long as myriads of conversions are perforce made
One Christian is like another only a difference in name
Are tortured and maimed?
The Baptist distrust Lutherans and their God is the same
One believes the other should be shamed
Even Jews and the non-ordained by God were caught in the flame

Under the same heaven under the same sky
All the slaughtering and all the vying ended in reform?
God's empire became a triumvirate not a unity of one?
Which does God choose for his heavenly run?

What Is Sin?

What if a man is gay, but never has a tryst would he go to hell and sit on the devil's lap and give him a kiss?

What if he had only had one tryst -a slight indiscretion - would he, again, go to hell and sit on the devil's lap and give him a kiss?

What about several trysts, would he, again, go to hell and sit on the devil's lap and give him a kiss?

Would many do the trick and, no doubt, those Christians finally howl, and cheer with bliss, "put him in hell and make him sit on the devil's lap and give him a kiss."

But how many trysts does it take to make a devil's fist?

Between desire and deed when does sin set in?

If he's gay and never acts and attends church and asks forgiveness, is he entitled to God's grace?

Would the Christians accept him as their own if only the urge takes place?

Is it the temptation or the act that is a disgrace?

If he imagines these trysts but never once for the eyes to bare, are these sins he must declare? -

Endless thoughts that come to bare but not one does he share.

Do endless temptations without the deed make a sin to be?

If they are only thoughts, is it enough for heaven's fee? -

A mere seed of a sin stuck in the bin, no need to worry or fret within?

Until it blooms into a deed pay no heed - desire all you need as long as it is only a dream?

So, it might be said, instead, keep it confined to the mind so only God can malign?

But He will bless you in kind as long as he remains sexless in time?

Does this free the sinner from his sin if I he keeps all his fantasies and desires within?

Will the Christian abide by this inclination?

What if he sins, and confess them before and never sins again is he entitled to God's libation?

What if a desire escapes its prison cell and becomes a deed to tell?

He rations his sins but confesses each time and dies in a sinless state?

Is he endowed with mercy and enters God's estate?

How many sins does it take to be notched upon the devil's stake?

How many must accrue before a soul must takes due?

When can the first stone be tossed and the self-righteous hear the first moan?

If I covet my neighbor's wife in my fantasies and dreams is this a sin?

Or take the Lord's name in vain in my brain does this, too, merit the same stain?

What if I utter it in a whisper so as not to offend my fellow man, is this the same with equal blame?

Would ten times aloud guarantee me a devil's shroud?
If I swore it every day would the heat of hell be worse than once or twice?
Would God be proud
When the devil pulled the throttle and burned the sinner to a crisp with His indignant frown?
When is a sin really an indiscretion that can't be undone? –
Deserves a good scolding from a nun.
Is a serial rapist who kills his victims enough to shun the man from heaven? -
Even if he asks to be forgiven?
A sinless man commits adultery and fails to confess before he dies -
The devil takes his hand
A serial rapist is heaven bound if he asks for forgiveness before he dies -
God takes his hand.
If the Sabbath is missed once or twice
Or missed, a hundred times the punishment would be the same for each vice.
If a man covets his neighbor's wife once is this enough to make the devil pounce?
If a man seeks forgiveness after coveting his neighbor's wife many times
Does God grant him a shrine?
Sinners can be redeemed in heaven's eye for all eternity
A holy man can be denied heaven's gate with the devil's grin of posterity.
One lie without forgiveness is far worse than many lies taken with every breath
If forgiveness is sought before death.
A compulsive liar who seeks forgiveness is far better off in the eyes of the lord
Than the poor man who lied once and dies before atonement.
The amount of suffering meted out for sin is never clear.
One sin without redemption can be a curse far worse than the sins of wretched murderer.
Punishment for sin is as unclear as a frothy stream.
One sin or many sins it is all the same to Him -
No way to know the dictum or protocol for judging God's whim.
Is heat of hell for one unforgiven sin the same for many unforgiven sins?
Why should the devil's hand be as hot for a meagre sinner as for a habitual sinner?
Heaven is littered with egregious sinners
And hell harbors the sinless without a hopeful glimmer.

Ode to Virginity

Take pride in holding out
Maintain your virginity without hesitation or doubt
Be a virgin until your wedding night -
Remain as pure as Snow White.
Avoid masturbation – it's a ploy
God will be annoyed
Watching you fondle your favorite toy
Exterminating your next of kin quicker than a henchman.
A veritable slaughter with each ejaculation.
Resist this sin - you'll become a simpleton.
If you love Jesus and you hear his heavenly call
By all means resist the temptation to fondle your balls
When you step up to bat –
Skip that awful habit.
Save it when you cohabitate - strike the ball and resist that temptation.
If prayer fails to quell those prurient urges within
Consult a guru and try a little Zen,
Chanting with prayer beads is another way to win
Beware - consulting with non-Christians is another sin.
Flagellation might be best
To vanquish any illicit unrest -
Whip away and until you past the test
And the desire is fully suppressed.
Besides, Jesus might blush
To see a man, make such a fuss,
Fondling his loins with such a delightful lust,
Moaning and groaning joyfully with every imaged thrust.
Shed the wonder lust - let it go - the pleasure is a bust.
Long for a turtledove you can call your own
That no one else has ever boned,
Hope her hymen wasn't unsown
So, she won't need to atone -
Avoided those first moans
When her virtue could be stolen,
Or be at risk for an Islamic stoning.

Someday your princess will come
And you can stop being abstinent and cum.
Fondle her bosom and have some fun -
You've earned it- go ahead and succumb.
Tell your lover that she's the first you've ridden -

Hope she's not a tart that dabbled in the forbidden
And blooded her sheet
With her first sexual feat.
We must be discrete
Hold back our passions so Jesus will be up-beat -
Mutual virgins - declare we are in intact.
We need not despair
If neither one had an affair -
God's law has made us a perfect pair.
We remained abstinent and curbed our lust -
We didn't let our desires make us nonplussed -
We resisted those sensuous tempests that might cause a fuss
And turned to Jesus when it got tough.
Rest assured I endured- never screwed on the cuff,
Hope she can claim the same and it's not a bluff -
It might be tough
To avoid being a heathen who has already cummed -
Hope she held out - a heavenly stunt,
And lived like a celibate monk -
And had her first orgasm as a virgin - not as a slut.

God is our coxswain – a sexless love blessed by a chaplain
We virgins can proclaim.
From the altar we're entitled to become a beacon and explain
To future virgins filled with passion - you aren't to blame.
It's the devil's plan to turn her into a concubine
Or tempt him to be a John roaming the streets for a lustful opine -
Yield to those cocksure urges -that's His aim!
Consent to the pagan's canon that wants to set those desires aflame!
Pray hard! Take cold showers! Curb the lust that's in the loins
Train them to refrain -
Be celibate lovers who can sustain
The carnal strain
Until the sheets are rightfully stained.
Crusade for purity -
Maintain a rigorous piety,
Avoid acceding to those sensuous desires brazenly -
Virginity is proof of love the angels espouse sternly.
And Jesus reveres firmly.
An untouched vulva is a God's gift He won't resend –
It's a gift to men even if they have sinned -
At least one can ascend.
Once the hymen is torn – nothing is left to amend -

Repenting with a prayer can't end with an amen.
Who wants a woman after many men –
After she's committed an egregious sin.
An untouched member is the same -
Keep it flaccid avoid God's shame.
Don't hide your remorse and claim the maid is too blame -
Man up! - remain a virgin all the same,
Find a worthy lass that hasn't been defamed -
Mutual virgins can transcend
And be with God without end -
Don't lift your skirt or unbutton your fly
And rub each other's thigh;
God's grace is hard to come by.

Lust and love don't mix
Unless a whore your eyes do fix – then resist
Find a virgin and hump with divine intent,
With a vestal mate that won't dissent
To a lustful intent with God's consent -
Resisted having her virginity spent.
Now she can moan and groan and not repent
God will celebrate the event
When a stain of blood is on the sheet –
Another virgin down - holy and discreet.
Get a ring and gal untouched
Who avoided penetration as her holy task -
Toss the rest who are unmatched.
Their morality is inflated -
Their virginity confiscated
Their lust was consummated
before it was venerated.
God knows the virgins who were consecrated
And those who were desecrated.
Without a ring don't dabble when you're captivated.
Don't' claim to be a born-again virgin -
It won't work –
God will think you're a jerk.
Resist that scorn – stay a virgin the minute you're born.
Don't open your legs for any bloke
Or use a dildo for a pleasing stroke.
Disguise that bulge in your pants.
Don't beat it off at every chance.
Shove those urges aside - look askance,

Stay a virgin it's your best chance,
Give up on that sensuous romance,
Stifle those urges –
Relish instead those Godly surges.
Kissing and fondling may be okay
As long as the genitals aren't on display,
Touch lightly – don't get aroused and betray your wedding day -
Make no sensuous blunders that might offend Yahweh.
Let loose on your wedding night it's the divine way
God permits your bulge to be seen at last -
Fondle it rigorously until it is no longer downcast
Whisper a prayer and put it on display
With those moans and groans, endeavor in foreplay,
Don't hold back no reason to slack
As long as you keep the Sabbath -
You've earned your whirl wind of lust and passion
Just keep Jesus in mind when you orgasm.
He'll appreciate the thought
"Panting and lust can go hand in hand with God's grace", He'll remark.
To those who saved their lust for the wedding march.
With a ring and a priest God condones carnality -
He'll make no accusations of immorality
Or show partiality -
Liberate those lecherous urges of abandoned sexuality!
God will relish your divine lust
If you dress your Sunday best
And cease having that bulge in your pants
Abstain this one day let God have his way
Resume coitus the next day –
All that lustful moaning and fondling can wait.

The virgin life can be lived without strife or lace
As long you stare upon her face;
Keep your thoughts steady and pray for grace -
Don't look between her legs -you'll be staring at Satan's face.
God gave you these urges to suppress
So be His guest -show him you can repress.
Carnal thoughts are here to stay but buck up before they debase.
Genuflect, grab the rosary, stay a virgin - keep up the noble fight,
Heaven's yours if you can hold off an orgasm until your wedding night,
Then blast away - you're entitled to a respite.
God won't mind so satisfy that appetite.
Virginity is part of God's divine plan

A covenant between God and man;
Keep it in your pants- be as strong as Tarzan
And put your faith in God's hands
And let it spring forth on your wedding night.
If you bag a virgin before your wedding night
Resist deflowering her with all your might,
Making a conquest of a virgin isn't right -
It's callous-like a cowboy notching his belt
With prideful spite.
Marry a virgin and make it right
Make heaven your ultimate plight.
Avoid deflowering her – don't commit that ultimate crime
Don't taste the wine before its time
Don't drink the keg before the party's begun.
Hang on - make allegiance with God and a virgin
Get it when its right –
His eyes will grow bright.
Let Him be a voyeur –
Nodding with virtuous approval.
Maintain your scruple
And fornicate when it's time
That way you'll shine.
What could be more pleasing than two virgins intertwined? -
Copulating for the divine?

The Crucifix

D'Amoto and Helms were quick to toss
Serrano into Satan's flame.
The masses soon followed with threats and blame -
bomb the museums - kill the man with that cursed name –
who made his fame-
submerging a plastic Jesus in urine -
how lame and without any shame.
When Jesus was in the Holy Land,
he wasn't averse to stand
and raise his frock
and piss on a rock.
This desert leak stirred up a little dust,
but one made a fuss
when he took that piss
in front of the apostles and nothing went amiss;
poor Jesus – He had no Honey Pot to urinate in.
Local latrines were few and far between -
weren't readily available or very clean –
so, an open spray without delay
would certainly have made His day.

Seeking revenge
the Christians threatened to go on a killing binge –
a regular Jihad
in the name of God
to yank plastic Jesus from His pod
and vow to kill Serrano
and blow up his "Piss Jesus" statue
without reservation or a single miscue.
Treachery and hate were everywhere on que -
impossible to subdue.
Everywhere "piss Jesus" went
a noble crowd was sent -
pursuing a pious plot
to "Kill Serrano"
"Blow him up – he's got poor Jesus soaking in a pot!"
This upstanding lot
put poor Jesus in a spot
worse than Jesus soaking in a bottle of urine
or wiggling on a dash board rubbed with pee
and believe, in the wink of eye -

even if there's a sty -
everything is a heresy
that doesn't agree with God's self-righteous plot.

Many of those evangelicals are proud to display
their plastic Jesus on a suction cup.
No one complains when He's glued and stuck
wobbling like a divine bobble-head run amok
or shaking like a Hawaiian hula dancer on the dash board of a pickup.

Many believe that He shouldn't float in urine,
complaining it's a poor version – foreign for God's son.
But dash board Jesus is soaked with urine and sweat
after an affectionate fondle or a hearty grip.
Feces too is on His skin
from a dirty hand of a folksy ken
when he grabs his bobbing Savior
longing for redemptive favor.
A sweaty palm, none the less,
they'd have to confess,
is as bad as poor Jesus in a urine jar.
Mercury and lead also abide on his hide,
along with CFCs and sulfur dioxide.
He swirls and swings from side to side
resurrected every day
with his acrobatic skills on display,
while "Piss Jesus" sits quietly
in his little golden chamber,
pollutant free-except for a little pee.
Why make Him struggle as a hula dancer,
or wiggle back and forth like a party rapper
glued to dash board wobbling on a suction cup.
The question remains which should be shamed or held to be corrupt?
No matter which one bears fruit
there is no transcendent pursuit,
no angel playing a flute
no souls to persecute,
no transcendental place
for wayward souls to be displaced
because they were unchaste.

Jesus was a fetus once.
No one but a dunce could renounce

that He floated in a womb full of pee.
No one threatened God for not letting Him flee
From a womb full of pee -
Why shame poor Serrano for doing the same? -
keeping Jesus in a plastic uterine full of urine?
There was no call to arms against poor Mary
who let little Jesus tarry?
in her unconsummated womb full of urine.
Why shoot Serrano for imitating God's plan?
No one goes to church and raises an angry hand
and yells at God -
"Like Serrano, you let poor Jesus float in a womb full of urine!"
What hypocrisy!
To condemn a man who left Jesus
to reside peacefully in bottle of urine
for a contemplative moment
in a quiet museum
when others let Jesus bob on a dash board
like a hula girl twisting about
for all voyeur devotees to check out
or a sleaze to fondle after a quick squeeze.

No one chastises God for his grand scheme
of trapping poor Jesus in a piss-filled uterine,
while Serrano is threatened for the same scheme -
condemned to live in infamy when he did the same -
soaked poor Jesus in urine - only to be shamed.
Why hate Serrano?
Jesus never complained about the muck and grime
He endured in the womb -
swimming about in excrement and urine.
If Jesus didn't complain about God's plan,
why should we complain about Serrano's artistic elan?
Like Jesus, we took our turn resting in excrement
and floating in urine.
Not to worry –
If Jesus is safe in heaven after he pissed in a desert
and soaked it with urine
why become like Jihadists - thirsty for blood?
and drag poor Serrano through the mud,
blow up a museum like a common thug.
Serrano was trying to be holy
not intending to raise an eyebrow or two

when he put a plastic Jesus in a tube of pee-
a holy gesture that imitated God's plea –
sent His son to prevent mankind's sins to fester
while trapesing about took a good pee in the desert.
He didn't intend to mock the hordes
or goad a self-righteous posse to mount their steeds
and go on a killing spree.

He was averse to start a crusade
or starving for an accolade.
They should let him have his artistic decree
and see that Jesus had no qualms soaking in pee.
After all, He is the son of God and pushed away a rock
and fled to heaven to be with his flock
no longer soaking in pee.
We all thrived in a womb full of urine -
Why be so holy and sanguine?

Serrano put Jesus in a bottle of pee
so, the world could see
the sacrilegious role Christians play-
how they desecrate Jesus with their token display
of petty rituals and witless bigotry -
far worse than Jesus in a jar of pee.
They piss on Jesus with their holy charades
and their perfidious tirades
make penitents feel condemned
even torture and kill for their end.

The Will of God

Voltaire astutely asked
After Lisbon was taken to task
Was God careful to select the innocent from the depraved -
The good from the bad?
The apparent caprice in the selections He made –
Sparing the wicked and punishing the good –
Makes redemption for sin misunderstood.
If evil is secured and grace is obscured –
It's unclear what punishment gains,
Or what it explains
When children are crushed or buried alive,
And humble servants don't survive,
God's whimsical nature seems to thrive.
Humility is best He behests –
Buck up and accept the tortuous test -
Trust my punitive choices.
Are benevolent miracles just a jest
Undeserving we are pursuing a foul quest;
But how can that be when injustice isn't addressed?
Burying children was high on His list
Rape and pillaging are what He seemed to bless.
How does this steer us from sin?
Goad us to seek redemption when we can?
Inspire us to seek His loving hand?
When barbaric acts are His to demand.
How are we to trust God
When His ruthless deeds are a façade -
Claims the undefiled – how odd
And spares the culpable – what a fraud!
If we claim that God knows best
Then we must be pests
Who deserve to live in this punitive unrest.
Perhaps more suffering is a test;
Our pleas for redemption go unheeded -
More evil is what is needed! -
Spare us any benevolent miracles.
Pain and sin are the ploy
We should jump with joy
And accept these malevolent ways
And grant His diabolical enterprise our praise.
His creatures are permitted any act that tests his love

Take your pick it comes from above –
Child molestation, rape, extermination, infidelity - an evil pileup!
A host of choices that sacrifice innocent victims
In order to tempt His creatures to sin -
All to gain or lose His love.
These temptations risks children and the righteous to gain eternal life.

We can't question His wisdom and seek his advice.
We must forfeit our understanding of his punitive ways
And turn away -
Give Him the benefit of the doubt and simply pray
His direful maze of torture -imbued in nature and in man –
isn't leading us astray.
We insist in loving Him anyway
Even if a child is raped and killed to test His love –
We must honor this deed of temptation from above.
To see if the sinner would fail or run -
Willing to sacrifice a child for a divine hunch.
Cruelty is necessary to for God's plan
It's His way to redemption -
Benevolence is an exemption.
The child was God's sacrificial lamb -
Accept his proclamation - "That's who I am".
We gain heaven if we don't question these malevolent ways
Bound for hell if we abhor these diabolical ills.
No! More sacrifice and punishment are needed from above.
Nail a man to a cross – a sadistic crumb for us bums –
A hollow option instead of love.
Manifest plagues and polio too
Not to mention a disease or two
That extends our suffering and has no cure.
Birth defects, painful as they are, designed to punish the pure –
Makes us into worthy supplicants begging for a cure.
But some contend that God knows best
And evil is necessary to cause unrest -
We can mold ourselves with every test.
God created heaven and earth
Thought it best to cast it in dearth
Create an abundance of gratuitous pain
Distributed it in a heartless bane.
He thought it best to offer us His brutal hand -
It was His inexorable Plan
To degrade our souls for a lifespan.

It is a clever and devious design –
No need to protest the divine
We may be mystified by the evil deeds He oversees -
Or be discontented in the way He has to be pleased
But we are stuck with His undeniable wisdom
Or his misplaced vision of dispensing pain
Without other options to proclaim -
Love, compassion, benevolent miracles –
Seems He ignores a benevolent Kingdom,
And overlook God's denial of other selections -
Accept unprecedented suffering –
Without a compassionate nod –
As the wise and word of God.
God's prerogatives are His own -
Why pain is meted out - regardless of virtue or grace –
Even to those who consume the host and sip the golden chalice -
Often winners in God's eye and destined for the sky
Are selected to be crushed and despised -
Remains His secret we can't question.
Why the ruthless are spared – those sinners who never complied -
Even winked and smiled -
Gratified by their reprieve.
Rapists, thieves, ruthless dictators, child molesters -
All coddled and spared - never attended vespers -
Granted, it seems, absolution and mercy.
Perhaps we think they'll get theirs in the second coming –
Punishment is around the corner we proclaim.

Why children were raped and tortured -.
Sacrificed in hideous ways
While and sinners were set free Is a mystery.
Surely, He'll justify why children of Auschwitz heard no lullaby –
Smothered and baked in ovens unidentified -
Their bones mixed with kin and ancestors alike.
Why a child was swept from her bed one lonely night,
Raped and tortured and skinned alive in horror and fright.
Was this necessary for transcendent heights? -
Only God knows – that will have to suffice.
The plague nearly extinguished the race
He'll surely explain why this was so base –
Necessary for a transcendent place.
Why diseases like dystrophy the "suicide disease",
Ebola - easy to spread - internal bleeding until the victim is dead,

Lesch-Nylan syndrome –
A victim of a corrupt chromosome.
A God ordained mutation -
Nothing can be done - a real vexation.
Severe spasms and self-mutilation -
Try praying – for God's intervention
Before death puts an end to this painful emasculation.
Put CJD on the list
Another disease that can't be dismissed
No cure or reason – an incurable feast
That leads to dementia and death -
One of God's gems when He created the heaven earth!
Driven insane with holes the brain -
Lapses into a coma
Before it turns fatal and lays its painful claim.
God's malevolent plan is on display -
with Brainerd Diarrhea in full array.
Etiology unknown, a cure postponed -
Cheer up! – God might intervene – it's possible to survive this one
After months with fecal incontinence that can't be undone.
God is at his relentless best with Fatal Insomnia -
Sleepless nights with dementia and paranoia
Not to mention annoying hallucinations
Until a coma precedes death.
Congenital diseases are difficult to explain
Malformations of the most hideous kind
Plague the purest of mankind.
Heart defects, brain anomalies, with the added attraction of deformations -
Limbless bodies, facial clefts, blindness –
God's freak show to entertain us.
Prince Randian the snake man -
Gave a great limbless sideshow – on demand.
Ella Harper the Camel Girl -
Who couldn't twirl -
Pleased the crowd when she walked on all fours.
Frank Lentini with his parasitic leg
Earned a lot of money and didn't have to beg.
Myrtle Corbin was better yet
Had two pelvises and four legs poking out of her skirt.

Hold tight to the divine
Have faith God will explain
How this suffering is necessary despite all the pain

And all these sacrifices in this Name.
It's one thing not to blame
And accept all this suffering in his Name
When we correct these infamous shame
Are we interfering with God's undisclosed plan?
Finding remedies to curb God's divine machinations? -
A sinful jest on our part to interfere with benevolent intentions
Leaving us perplexed - which ones are permitted to correct?
Which disease is necessary for redemption?
Which ones not? -there's no way to tie this uncertain knot.
God blindly tosses out so much suffering and pain
It's hard to sort through the ones we need
Which ones to defer –
This is a costly affair! -
Which ones are we to claim?
Which one to leave unclaimed? -
So God can resume His unexplained pain
And we can resume celebrating God's heavenly plan -
Better off with the Black Death, measles, malaria and tuberculosis?
Were we wrong in the finding cures?
God must have a reason for all these sordid affairs
After all, they were designed to enrich our souls -
Makes us strive for supernal goals
Ending the scourges may be a disgrace
How do we know it's our place?
And remain in His good grace
Vaccinations for polio and tetanus -
Which one are we to efface?
That He would embrace?
Were we wrong ending these scourges? –
It ended much suffering that wasn't needed
God's plan that should've gone unheeded?
Whatever the case
We need to cease being a menace
His cruelty is not a blemish – it's for our penance.
Plagues and devasting earth quakes are for the Good –
Don't bother putting much stock in this sadistic illusion –
Nothing but senseless effusion.
Show God we agree with His conclusion.
We need to toss any doubting Thomas into the sea
Who think God is cruel or effete!
Doubters can't be at peace
Unless these accusations cease.

Even if God's horrific scheme might leave us perplexed,
We must remain faithful rather than vexed.
God is omnipotent – wouldn't punish us unless we needed it.
Be of good cheer retribution with a tear -
Curse benevolent miracles – live a life of despair!
We are better off with the Black Death, measles, malaria and tuberculosis
Think kindly of rapists – God put them here to test our love for him.
Despair when we find a cure for another blight -
They were put here for our redemptive delight,
Designed to enrich our souls,
He's not a mass Murderer –
Millions have died senseless deaths on His behalf
We need to belie those many epitaphs
He has his reasons for all these diseases
Has benevolent motives for these devastating earthquakes
Cease these diatribes that questions God's plan!

Tomb of Time

We gather lost souls at the tomb of time
Desperate for the sublime
Before we hear the chime from the shadow of death
Clairvoyant time precedes our final breath
And smiles-a prescient and cynical smile-at our brief digress
As warriors redress with their sanctimonious behests.

Religion is the concubine for the sublime
A cuckold if you will for fools who have an inkling to malign
The profane and cast the first stone
Makes no difference if they writhe in pain or groan
They must atone!
They must atone!

The sacred is the rule of thumb
To cast the stone and yell "The scum!"
Love is not far from their lips
Self-righteous creeds mark the eclipse
And sanctify the deeds and bless the interdict
Ascension with a smile after the apocalypse.
There is no shame in mocking the profane
As long as Jesus's blood is sustained
And another crusade can purge the land
And save mankind
From dissenters who won't repent
From malcontents who refuse to relent.

There is no shame in going amok
Let the blood ooze like a flood
In the clefts of dirt and mud
Leave the sinner's corpses for vultures and bugs.
Redemption is the creed
For these war mongering deeds.
In the name of the Father and the Son and the Holy Ghost-
Consume the host
And hang their heads on the bloody posts.
Liberation from retribution comes with the Pentecost
God smiles from his abode-
Left to dote when more are smote.
The killing fields of yesteryear
Are silent now after the interlocutor

Of nail and thesis and God's hand avowed with cheer
To drain blood for many a sepulcher.
Massacred in droves for their rightful heirs?
The Pope in Rome and God in Heaven the cross to bear?
Those who refused obeisance to either two did despair after the accord
Were sliced in parts by many a kindly Christian sword
Stacked like cairn At St. Lambert's church to scorn- a pagan's feast to behold!

To mend the wounds of bloody treachery and further religious zealotry
A wedding and massacre were set to celebrate an apostle's day,
Who saw Christ's ascension and could not stray!
Yet hatred sparked the resolute and tyrannical foray.
That beckons to the conscience that even God can't repay.
And questions persist to this day
Which side did God want slaughtered in the zealot's fray?
Did heavens weep or celebrate at the Calvinist's massacre?
Or praise and dance at the best Catholic executor?

Did a divine wand touch the souls of those who slaughtered the most?
Fought the hardest to perpetrate the bloody Pentecost?
Which did God appreciate the most-
Anabaptists' bleeding body parts decomposing in cages
The Huguenots' corpses floating in the Seine
Or putrefying in the streets after the Parisian purge?

Perhaps Satan is to blame
The scape goat for every vile act of shame
Coaxed these persecutors of Christ to rend and slice for fame
But God can sort through those acts of vicious acclaim
Heaven is secured for those who massacred without intention to inflame
The Redeemer's mercy is a fleabane
That determines the noble slayers from ignoble ones.
The merciful executioners from the cruel puissant ones.

Exterminate, humiliate the inhuman beasts- the Huguenots are to blame
Let the carrions devour the corpses of the slain.
Let the Seine wash them away and leave no stain-
Baptism of the dead; His will be sustained.
Militant sermons sanctioned by God will redeem any deed.
For the Redeemer's sake heresy has to be restrained
Torture, maim fight to gain a monopoly on hate.
As long as it's won with a purity of heart.

Does God take mercy on this murderous rage
As long as myriads of conversions are perforce made
Christians becomes Christians only a difference in name
Earned the right to be tortured and maimed?
Even Jews and the non-ordained by God were caught in the flame
Under the same heaven under the same sky
All the slaughtering and all the vying ended in reform?
God's empire became a triumvirate not a unity of one?
Which does God choose for his heavenly run?

The nail and thesis of God's hand avowed with cheer
To drain blood for many a sepulcher.
Massacred in droves for their rightful heirs?
The Pope in Rome and God in Heaven the cross to bear?
Those who refused obeisance did despair
Were sliced in parts by many a kindly Christian sword
Stacked like cairn At St. Lambert's church to scorn-
A pagan's feast to behold!

To mend the wounds of bloody treachery and further religious zealotry
A wedding and massacre were set to celebrate an apostle's day,
Who saw Christ's ascension and could not stray!
Yet hatred sparked the resolute and tyrannical foray.
That beckons to the conscience that even God is reluctant to repay.
And questions persist to this day
Which side did God wants to slaughter in the zealot's fray?
Did heavens weep or celebrate at the Calvinist's massacre?
Or praise and dance at the best Catholic executor?

Did a divine wand touch the souls of those who slaughtered the most?
Fought the hardest to perpetrate the bloody Pentecost?
Which did God appreciate the most-
Anabaptists' bleeding body parts decomposing in cages
The Huguenots' corpses floating in the Seine
Or putrefying in the streets after the Parisian purge?
Coming from the shadow of death
Where they were deprived
Perhaps Satan is to blame
The scape goat for every vile act of shame
Coaxed these persecutors of Christ to rend and slice for fame
But God can sort through those acts of vicious acclaim
Heaven is secured for those who massacred without intention to inflame
The Redeemer's mercy is a fleabane

That determines the noble slayers from ignoble ones.
The merciful executioners from the cruel puissant ones.

Exterminate, humiliate the inhuman beasts- the Huguenots are to blame
Let the carrions devour the corpses of the slain.
Let the Seine wash them away and leave no stain-
Baptism of the dead; His will be sustained.
Militant sermons sanctioned by God will redeem any deed.
For the Redeemer's sake heresy has to be restrained
Torture, maim fight to gain a monopoly on hate.
As long as it's won with a purity of heart.

Does God take mercy on this murderous rage
As long as myriads of conversions are perforce made
Christians becomes Christians only a difference in name
Earned the right to be tortured and maimed?
Even Jews and the non-ordained by God were caught in the flame
Under the same heaven under the same sky
All the slaughtering and all the vying ended in reform?
God's empire became a triumvirate not a unity of one?
Which does God choose for his heavenly run?

The Vision

Joseph Smith and Brigham Young
Had a vision and spoke in tongues -
Jesus took flight from heaven,
And went to Connecticut
To roam America to find a settlement.
Utah was a place
They could have sex
With multiple wives –
What a deal -
Ordained by God;
Yet the trinity was cast under the rug,
As accusations of being deviant thugs
Prompted them to pull the plug
On group sex with loved ones.
Jesus didn't mind,
But they still opined
That diddling more than one
Had to be declined –
Even if stateside Jesus didn't malign.
How ideal –
This divine deal -
A harem without a kuffiyeh.
God ordained this sensuous yoke –
It's certainly a lucky stroke!

When Jesus came stateside,
All other religions aside,
The true church came to reside.
All those fools before were to be derided
The Mormons testified   -
Spiritual narcissism denied -
They were the only ones God recognized.
Baptism wasn't required,
Unless sinners are dead and ready for heaven,
And they had departed from Eden -
Missouri's haven -
And gave up being heathens.
God is our loving Heavenly Father;
In His name they didn't bother
With all the evil that did follow.
When prophets and apostles –

Without a hint of sorrow -
Ordered the faithful to murder and massacre,
By the Mormon militia,
Those who didn't adhere to their beliefs;
Even innocent immigrants who tried to retreat –
The Mountain Meadows slayings was such treat -
They needed saving for blood atonement,
For their heavenly attainment;
To atone, blood must be shed
Upon the ground -
A sacrificial offering for those who fouled,
As those Mormons who scowled,
Blamed native Americans for their treachery
To maintain their wicked solidarity -
Exterminating gentiles occupying the Holy Land of Missouri.
Whether Jesus was in the US or Jerusalem,
They murdered and tortured like other good Christians -
Typical of their self-righteous vision.
Even rape was consensual sex -
Women were slaves to be raped –
Guilty of being unchaste and tempting to men -
Mormon men cried amen!
Women are sinners - never chaste! -
Take them without haste.

LDS believe in their holy lot,
Blessed by Jesus a veritable Camelot
Take Lafferty - a loyal Mormon
Anxious to reform -
Had a revelation from God to perform,
And slash the throats of his sister-in-law,
And her one-year-old without a flaw.
Bundy too was a converted Mormon -
What a misfortune -
Committed thirty homicides -
A serial killer without a tear in his eye,
Or a hint of remorse or a sigh.
Franklin was another holy kin -
A racist and another serial killer
Known to embrace
The execution of those who threatened his race.
Bishop was a devout Mormon,
An Eagle Scout and a pedophile,

Who like child-pornography -
Molesting and slaying young boys – a hideous biography.
Mark Hoffmann was a killer, a forger and a bomber -
Another Mormon Without a speck of honor.
Evril LeBaron took underaged girls to be wives,
And set out to kill anyone he despised –
A blood covenant to kill those who didn't comply
Family or spy – they had to die.
Jodi Arias murdered her Mormon womanizer,
Stabbing the unmarried man in a shower –
Not before he was her baptizer.
Huntsman killed six of her newborns -
One after the other as they came out of the womb -
Stored them in the garage;
No one knew of this perfect sabotage,
Until she made quite a stir -
Her husband did concur -
When she left their remains behind,
After she moved to gain peace of mind.
MacNeil killed his wife,
And sodomized and raped his daughter.
Killpack killed her child for stealing Kool-Aid;
Served only six years for torturing and drowning her child -
She claimed she's reformed -
No more 'water intoxication' deaths to morn,
Especially for her natural born.
Jared Padgett so devout,
He was a deacon at twelve - so proud -
Until, at fifteen, he committed suicide,
After he gunned down a fellow student.
Stateside Jesus wasn't prudent
Lacked divine jurisprudence.

Perhaps Mormon scriptures revoke violence -
Eschews the fury of nihilists.
When the pages are turned,
And ideas are spurred,
It's a pagan worship of war,
Decapitation and dismemberment and ecclesiastical valor -
Divinely sanctioned violence – a spiritual dagger.
The stateside Jesus proclaims
Sinners walk the plains,
And everyone else Latter-day-Saints disdain

Need to be set in flames -
Especially If they aren't Mormons.

The Mormon prophesy was written on golden plates
And buried in New York state
Hidden In a stone box
After Moroni said it wasn't a hoax,
And tooted his horn,
And stole them so they wouldn't be adorned –
No one saw them except in a dream
Best Joseph could swear so it seemed.
This vision had more to be sworn
When he suddenly appeared in Brazil,
Prophesizing he was the host
Of these Golden Plates -
What a tale of hide and seek,
When Jesus appears in Missouri and then Brazil, as well;
Perhaps it won't be long He'll appear in Louisville!
Written on golden plates
Buried in New York
In a stone box
After Moroni said it wasn't a hoax.
And tooted his horn
And stole them so they wouldn't be adorned.
But Joseph Smith appeared in Brazil
Said he was the host
Of these Plates -
What a tale of hide and seek.

Shadows of Time

Lost in the shadow of time
Those forgotten souls
Who wrote no scrolls,
Or deserved to be extolled.
Praised only for their roles,
Victims of Nazi stoves
Buried in mass graves -
The slimy mud
Soaked with their blood.

No one knows
Those lost souls -
Their convulsive bodies -
Their dried bones
After the plague
Eclipsed their lives.
Lost to the centuries -
Anonymous memories.

All those Huguenots
Tossed in the Seine
Forsaken in sin
By those with a pious spin -
Forgotten corpses
Thoroughly drenched
By the French -
Massacres kept the Catholics entrenched.

The myriads of soldiers
In trenches of squalor -
A paradise for lice
Where their feces preside.
They paid the price
of torture and sacrifice -
headaches and painful rashes
fevers and relentless scratching -
tossing ubiquitous feces in every direction.
A feast for parasite aggregation.

A bullet to the head
A bayonet to the chest

While Typhus fever took care of the rest -
Lethal pneumonia progressed
Adding to lethal conquest.

Ocean bound -
Lost and never found.
Eaten by salt –
The ocean's tongue.
Their bones rattle
Against the mettle shell –
The womb of death
That sways in the current
Like a child's cradle.

How many have perished
Myriads of nameless faceless banished
In the shadow of time
Not even a gravesite to call their own.
Their birth unbeknown

The sun shines
On all those shadows
In sod and dirt
From miscreant deeds
And nature's will -
God ordained? - Its evil shrill
Echoes through the ages,
A mystery for sages.

Flowers of Evil

I uncovered your love
It was and stark -
eaten away by hate - shunned by the Lark.
Alas,
I saw the falsity
in your grandiosity
And your claims of rightful inequality –
Entitlement to heaven's prize
The rest are despised
No matter how wise
Or good nature apprized,
You deem unwise -
Sinners you chastise.

You tried to claim my love
And pawn me off as an earthly blotch
to gain a heavenly notch.
For you are the pawnbroker of souls -
That spawn
The Savage Feast of scions.
Compassion is not the theme –
Chicanery is the scheme
for buying and selling souls
Auctioned off to highest bidder
For those you could deliver,
Devout and chaste without a sinful quiver
The rest are left to wither.

You defend with the cross and sword! -
Ignoring those victims for centuries who lay bloody in the sward,
Sacrificed in the deadliest of atrocities
For ignoring Yahweh's Word -
Sixteen million were slaughtered
In the name of the Lord.
Their throats slashed
Their tongues removed - vocal castration,
A Pentecostal purgation.
It's easy with minister's weary and resolute claw -
Facilitate climbing over the Garden Wall
And kill those who stall
And rebel against that sinful fall –

Refuse to comply to that self-righteous call.

Does God forgive
This mayhem and carnage?
And hold you in divine bondage
Make a bargain for your womb
To plant the seeds of doom
For you to cultivate those Flowers of Evil.
That can be listed with their deadly charm –
Those children who will flourish and do harm
Like the sweet buttercup –
the "Devil's Helmet" or the "Monkshood" –
They threaten the sinner with toxic rhetoric of doom.
Love Jesus and fires of hell will never loom -
Let another sinner take your heated room.

The seductive "Hooker's Lips" gives logic the slip,
So, they can plead their case in the thoughtless eclipse -
Seduce you to avoid the sinful abyss
And the Savior hard to dismiss -
Bread and wine will make for a Sunday feast,
A picnic that will be hard to resist.
This child will angle and twist
A heartfelt script.

The "Fangs of Dracula" with its venomous bite,
And the charm of Oculata with its ghastly stench
will make dissenters flinch
If they refuse to budge an inch -
Torment the sinner with hell's stench
And Satan's ruthless bite.

The "Snap Dragon Skull" can appall -
Remind those that death is for those
Who oppose salvation's repose,
But it's the Autumn Crocus-the "Naked Lady"- the most toxic child of all
Who will make sinners fear the fall,
If they dare not pray and be enthralled
By the tabernacle's enticing sham,
And swallow His Flesh and say "Amen".

These are the children
From the womb of redemption

Endowed in their heart
The covert flame of evil and deception.
Your seedlings nurtured
With the sunlight of hate
Glorified over and over with daily hymns of late
Thanked Pontius Pilot for giving them the gate -
With only rumor he did what they say
Put this unconsummated baby on a cross -
So he could push a rock
Declare He's here to save the flock
And those who follow the frock.
Heaven will be empty
Except the vigilantes -

Not many were saved -
Millions were left behind
Born of a consummated womb too soon
Or weren't asked to part of the flock -
Too far away to see a frock.

Incarnates of your seed
Ready to bloom
From Eden's deceptive gloom
When all the wretched creeds
did loom -
From ecclesiastical spume
And interbreed
And got dispersed
By those Flowers of evil
Turn reason into the demon -
Who disperse malevolence -
With unctuous smiles
United in picking out the vile
To condemn and defile
With their collusion and guile.

Fossils Don't Lie

We have a bond with the sea
Barebacked with salty loins
we made our way from muck and slime
To crawl upon the earth
To stay in huts and caves along the way.
We need not be dismayed
How it was we were creatures of the sea
And found our way to a stony hearth.
It rather trite to say we morphed
In seven days without a holiday -
Fingers, toes, knee and thigh
God pierced the sky
And with several shakes we complied
In the moon tide, made our sudden appearance -
Isn't a likely chance.
To manifest from nothing to something in an instant
An instantaneous world from heaven's enlistment
Without consummation, parents or offspring
Sinners and non-sinners in one big bag
Scoffers and pilfers - rapists, pedophiles, and murderers -
Quite a feat for seven days.
Without regret or a lot of sweat.
It's difficult to grasp such a lay out
When it's put to the test.
It's difficult for them to conceive,
We came from the sea,
No other way it can be gleaned –
Other assertions should be unweaned –
Mockeries of wisdom and should be demeaned.
Those blinders of religion should be unmasked;
It can't undermine transfiguration.
Or claim the earth is a few thousand years old
Each specie is like a statue unchanged and not foretold
Plopped here without genetic variation and endless nudity -
How embarrassing for God to see such mindless fecundity!
Unfavorable mutations are discarded or disband
The fit survive and not by God's hand -
A separate species ex nihilo is not in the plan,
Certainly not a divine elan –
A special species that's part of a providential clan.
A fairy tale is needed to bolster the case.

Where a porcupine and a man never die
Diseases are never on the sly.
But the redemptive apple did descry
And the fairy tale went awry -
Mere sinners that multiply
And man was put on a punitive standby -
For a sin they had no way to rectify.
And subject to death as the fly
If unfit for nature to qualify
Yet remain sacrosanct from evolution's eye.
Proclaiming all the while this not transcendent tittle tattle -
Or divine double talk,
When they profess that Eden is not a foolish committal
A mere fantasy - childish and incidental.
Insisting still, that man is a sinner condemned to hell
Subjected to diseases and any evil spell
But not evolution – that's the devil's evolving carousal!
Fall for that sinful temptation and God will bid you farewell.

Man was sent here by God's hand
Without a hint of transformation -
An unscathed species without a scratch on his back
Ready-made like the elephant in the zoo
Those skulls of Homo Erectus are Halloween masks -
Hard to ignore the Peking man -
This first flat face ancestor is not a fan
Or part of God's plan.
Perhaps He tossed it in
As a whim to forsake original sin.
To tempt sinners to become unhinged
With its precarious revenge -
Certainly, it will make them squirm
When the foresee evolution has an enticing charm.

The Neanderthal causes the quite an alarm
That weakens their aplomb.
Not us - but close enough
To cause a scuffle.
Did they have a Savior or an Eden
To prevent them from becoming heathens?
Which one does God curse?
Especially when four simultaneous species existed on earth.

Nine in all were replicas of us
Emerged from rock and sea
Did God make a fuss
Over which one to trust?
Call his own so he could torture his Son for us.
He'd be ashamed if he knew
The one he blessed was the worst of the crew
A warring species that liked to kill
And capture land at will.
Humans are part Neanderthal
For they did copulate and inbreed.
They gave us alleles to succeed
So, Jesus could become a divine Neanderthal.
Why are their such clues
We can peruse
Skulls and genes not our own
Transformed on our chromosomes -
Planted in our blood and bones
Not from Eden or God's throne.
We can account for all those boney faces
Unearthed like photographs
That render our cousins
That so offend.

Jesus Loves Football

Jesus likes to attend high scoring games
All those gladiators He wouldn't tame -
They send accolades in His name
For all their brutal gains
He'd never shame.
For they genuflect and blow kisses his way -
Hoping their adulations are not in vain
Their praises to His devotion to pain
Will let them win the game.

He receives those blown kisses heaven sent
Above the clouds for His consent,
Compares all those votive offerings
And deciphers, willingly, the merit of their groveling -
Weighing earnestly the savagery of their brutal offerings
To declare a winner for their brutality and pious jostling.
The players are certain its His intention
To listen to their prayers with rapt attention
No matter the severity of their aggression.
Kudos to you Jesus for letting me clobber -
Maim and hurt any man without a blocker –
What an honor! -
Watch me feast my eyes on a unsuspecting receiver
And send him reeling with that painful demeanor -
Laid out and ready for the coroner.
The game is delayed while everyone prays
And watches as he's wheeled off on a trolley cart –
Thumbs up – "Don't worry.   "I'll get a fresh start" –
"When I get off this cart."
"May never walk but I'm not dead."
"I'm only a retread."
"Sorry Jesus if I affect the point-spread."

When a spine or neck is broken
The teams go on one knee and pray he's not an omen -
Pray he'll get another chance get his neck broken,
Hope Jesus will listen to their sotto voce prayers that are softly spoken.
And takes any supplication as a token
And weighs their merit so potent
And blesses the injured player with motion.
Jesus must determine how hard they prayed

To see if the gurney bound man will be spared.
He favors these brutal omens
Prayers are abundant -
silent or spoken.

Even if He favors a brutal omen,
Whether their praises are offered silent or spoken,
Special dispensation is chosen
For those who are more earnest in their bosom
In genuflecting and blessing themselves with devotion.
It's an undisputed fact
Jesus loves football and broken backs.
The attention never slacks
When the quarterback is sacked
And comes up limping -
Those grateful prayers come bidding.
Those fans cheer and revere
Jesus's answers to a prayer
That enervates the player and ends his career
Without a tear or even a souvenir.
It's resolutely known
And it's not overblown
The team that elicits the most pain and wins
And broke all those limbs
Prayed a little harder to pull His strings.

Players like to hammer every opponents' head,
Rattle helmets until they're nearly dead
Crumbled up For Jesus's sake in a convulsive heap
Sanctifying every hit even if it's a little cheap.
Thanking the Lord for every crushing interception
And kneel in the end zone after that clever reception
And bend their head in grateful meditation.
Yes, Jesus loves football - garnering all the attention
Determines the outcome of each game by how hard they prayed.
The field goal kicker is quite the spade
Blesses himself before his skills are displayed.
If he misses, he can't explain
He blessed himself and made a prayerful campaign.
Perhaps, those imploring entreaties from the other team
Exceeded his divine claim.

Jesus has a tough decision
With all those imploring fans that want him to listen
And determine which team will glisten.

Players must wonder why their prayers were weak
And went unheeded when they used the same brutal technique,
Genuflected and pleaded with same imploring critique.
Weren't our brutal hits adequate to merit heaven's grace? –
We dealt many concussions and one hospital bound in disgrace.
Wasn't that good enough to merit His grace?
Didn't we grovel enough and elicit the required pain?
Pray on the sidelines before each brutal play?
Send helmets flying with hard-hitting blows
What did we do wrong that displeased you so?
Tells us what we must do to win so we aren't chagrined.
Do we lead with the head and injure the man instead?
Jesus please let us win - we'll be more brutal, cocky and bold
Like gladiators of old.
Remember, "Jesus loves ya man" when you make a hard hit
Snap a spinal cord or even a neck-
Put a man in a wheel chair with another lick,
Keep the faith and don't give up - Jesus might give you a break
Show up game day mean as snake
And favor your team the next bone crushing game you undertake.
Perhaps, He can put down a winner's stake -
If your team is commensurate in brutality.
Be more diligent with your prayers
And paralyze a player - this is what Jesus savors!
Fans and teams know that Jesus loves brutality
And the games head-knocking banality.
He is there Spokesman and Protector
Its Steward and its Savior -
Loves those prayer circles after the barbarity is over -
The genuflecting and signs of the cross.
Keep in mind faith can be kind
Jesus will favor your team next time
Let you win the next game of violent mediocrity.
If he can't, He'll flip a coin to judge such triviality.

Jesus on the Sidelines

C'mon Tebow its money and fame
that's your unbridled claim,
As you solicit Jesus's aid to gratify your aim.
It's battered brains and the Hall of Fame that's your game -
And God's support with your campaign
And the rigorous display of your Christian way.
In those coliseums you display your self-righteous sway -
Praying with Jesus supports your pagan play.
Your head bowed in a peaceful repose
Your trusty helmet by your side like a gladiator's pose
Or a crusader from a Holy War taking a bow
As the crowd erupts in a frenzied vertigo.
Soon your quiet meditation with Jesus ends
Time to pursue your violent aims that rarely offends;
Leading your men with chants or hymns,
When the whistle blows and the game begins.
Jesus comes to see Timmy play
And blesses those who kneel and pray.
Jesus is Tim's favorite friend
Believes his Savior will offer him a dividend -
And secure a win.
He doesn't need church to show his worth.
Tim's a virgin and loves to display

His sideline conversions -
Praying hardly before skulls are battered and bones are broken.
With many hard-hitting tokens
He genuflects before he maims his foe in Jesus' name
With gusto and fame.
Brain bashing and lethal blows to the body are okay
as long as they're done in the proper way.
Never lead with your helmet
Unless you can't help it.
Never get caught blindsiding a player -
A sure way to put him in a wheelchair.
A clip is to be avoided
Unless the ruthless deed can be exploited,
And the referee declines to call it.
These penalties may be verboten –
The red flag goes floating -
Unless the player has the ball – all bets are off –

Hit and mangle without being scoffed
That the given slogan
And Jesus might offer a token
And Timmy's fan won't be appalled -
Lay him out with utmost zeal and hearty blows –
And see if he waves his hand or wiggles his toes.
When he's carted off.

Crippled and numb a smile and a wave of the hand
Merits an applause from Timmy's fans -
surviving an attack certainly merits some slack -
even if Jesus has turned his back
and sides with his team's violent whack.
Who can resist this accolade? -
Even if it transgresses Timmy's crusade.
Who can't resist a player on a gurney?
He'll return after rehab - you'll see! - and endure more savage sprees.
He'll have more head-on-collisions and hear the roaring crowd.
Those titan hits, after all, do enthrall and bring no bloodshed or a brawl;
Players are laid to rest - out cold, starry eyed, concussion blessed.
Sideline vigils for these warriors' swift revival are the craze.
Injury-riddled prayer meetings with a foe warrant some praise.
Perhaps, Jesus would be pleased to see such a scene! -
Holy CTE boys joining Timmy on his knees,
Turning to their savior without shame -
Contrite and unashamed for playing such a brutal game.
Who can blame these "Born-Agains" for sneaking in a quick revival?
Serious injuries don't curtail brutal urges against Timmy's rival
And the spectator's love of savage travail.
The crusade resumes with aplomb;
Scantily dressed cheerleaders prance about
Like lap dancers at a strip club with every shout.
A little sex and lethal hits
While Timmy prays to Jesus for encouragement
Brings the blood thirsty crowd to its feet.
His team didn't always win, an inscrutable sin for some
A man with such connections should never be a victim;
He's a gallant warrior with a religious dictum.
But life is never fair even with a virgin with an earnest prayer -
God works in mysterious ways even for self-righteous player.
The conquerors always contend Jesus let them win;
Losers never say, as they whimper away, divine providence paved their way -
A sacrilege to proclaim Jesus dealt them an unfortunate end.

It's a one-sided game: winners benefit from Providence's helping hand -
But is oddly absent from blame
When the loser comes up lame.
A field goal is missed after a sigh of the cross
Does the kicker blame Jesus for the loss?
Swear and curse when the game was lost?
He prayed as hard as those at the Pentecost.
Win and Jesus gets a high-five or a friendly bump on the chin
Lose and He's coddled and the kicker takes the blame for a past sin –
Can't blame Jesus if other team's prayers had more steam.
When Timmy kneels on the sideline in prayer,
Holds one of his bench-clearing revivals -
Even for his rivals -
Did he pray for those laid to rest?
Beseech Jesus they be blessed?
Junior Seau gave his best but shot himself in the chest
when CTE set in.
Dave Duerson did the same –
put a bullet in his chest as a behest to autopsy his brain.
Mike Webster died in shame;
Dementia was to blame
After his induction into the Hall of Fame.
Was Jesus at their side
When they committed suicide? -
And pieces of their brain were put on a slide
And what was left showed how they died.

End-Game

Junior Seau did a good deed,
Shot himself in the chest instead of the head
To see if blows to the skull - helmet and all - left him dead.
Dave Duerson did the same -
He, too, shot himself in the chest rather than the brain,
So science could explain if CTE was to blame -
What a shame -
It turned out both were the same.
Brain slicing autopsies tell a lot
Especially if a brain is shot -
Full of hippocampus spots
Like rotten spots on an apple.
Those carved up little pieces for inventory -
Like slices of cauliflower rotting in a hopper -
Show the exploding imprint of a every crushing whooper
And the deadly frisson and slime and spit
before every hit.
The frontal lobe a battering ram
Took every slam
Until it quaked after every judicious wham.
To see such a sight made one cringe -
Just how many blows did impinge
Upon the brain and its fragile stem
To bring each man to their end
Like wilted roses in the summer sun.

"Iron Mike", tough as a spike, one of the Steeler's best,
Had, like the rest, too many pummels above the chest -
Numerous tau clumps left neurons and dendrites in distress.
Dead by fifty of dementia and dread, doctor Omalu said
"Was like twenty-five thousand car crashes laid on his head" -
"No wonder his brain was dead";
"There was nothing else his poor brain could sustain!"
He went on to proclaim.

John Grimsley shot himself cleaning his gun -
A ruse, pure and simple, to gain a catholic burial
But God knows best - he didn't really pass the Maryknoll test.
Nevertheless, his wife offered what was left
After he was put to rest - a votive offering for the dead.
Perhaps if all could see those amyloid plaques

From all those brutal contacts
God would waiver the suicide clause
And welcome him home without a pause.

Terry Long took out fraudulent loans
Committed arson
Ate rat poison
Before he settled on a gallon of antifreeze
To preserve his brain for those to see
If CTE is a disease.

Tyler Sash was dead at twenty-seven –
An instant exit to heaven
Drug toxicity preserved his brain
To show CTE had struck again -
Nestled in when he was quite young
Premature for one so young.
He had fewer hits than Seau -
Had the same -stage 2.

Ralph Wenzel drooled and mumbled away his final days
Absent-minded episodes lead him astray.
Took five years to bring about his demented end.
His brain harvested from the cremated flame
To see what was to blame for his fame
And those hallucinations they couldn't tame.

Andre Waters shot himself in the head;
We need not fret
Enough was left
After that 32-calibre slug
Was dug out of his head
To prove CTE wasn't inbred -
It was affirmed once again
A diced-up brain doesn't feign
When CTE lays its claim.

Jovan Belcher had CTE went on a killing spree
Shot his girlfriend nine times – a haunting decree.
With a deadly repartee
Shot himself in a parking lot
Next to a stadium where patrons pay a fee
To see those Titans parsing out those CTE's.

Helmeted gladiators pay a price -
What's left in their skulls will not suffice.
Gridiron dementia is the beatific prize
And lost memories of fame forgotten.
Were all those super bowl rings,
And all those pro bowl teams
Worth all those head busting stings
And those telltale red splotches on the brain?
When they gained all that fame? -
Worth a trip down Dementia Lane?
Perhaps the awards and accolades that heralded their names   -
Lured them to strive for that gridiron fame.
A Mecca of glory and fame –
A veritable warrior's world of brutality and disdain
A world where an assault was never a fault
And the cheers of the crowd sent them hurling in space -
Goaded them on to more crushing blows and deadly moans.
Silver sparks do fly when the brain is plastered on the fly -
Numb and tingling fingers, voices lingering, headaches, hallucinations
A golden glow like a laurel wreath upon the brow -
 Until the vision blurs.
Then the starry eyed-look with a blank and blink-less stare.
A few stingers here and there
And frightful head on collisions were fair.
Made it worth the praise
When they were in a haze -
It's not so bad that the brain shrinks in a daze
And withers into a chronic malaise
Memories and thoughts are fragmented like broken glass -
Fame and morass are one at last.
If dementia and fame are one in the same what's there to protest?
So why did Junior choose the chest?
To leave his brain to blame the game that gave him fame?
To convince his sons to peek at his brain
Before they're slain by this crippling game?
Still it needs to be pressed why he spared his brain and blew a hole in chest?
Did he have regrets that he paid such a debt?
Leave enough evidence to retaliate?
Or warn the men to come not to join the CTE club -
Avoid the paranoid fringe with no illumination within.
Wikipedia will share their fame
Will keep it lean
State their records and heroic deeds

Abbreviate their death to a date
Fail to state
That CTE was their curtain call.

Agnostic's Creed

Perhaps it's best to believe in God
We gain comfort and peace of mind,
Abandon our fears of retribution from the divine.
Faith is our tool
To be as naïve as any fool-
To accept the absurd
And be a convert
Of sin and degradation-
The right to castigate
With heartfelt persecution.
Deny any contradiction-
Even the invalid is made to fit-
No one cares that we are a dimwit.
We declare that God is transcendent-
Finger to the sky hoping He's got an eye-
An eternal spy on every little sin,
Answers our prayers and follows our thoughts.
Will listen to little children in PJs and socks,
Bowing in reverence- a supplicant's repose-
Hoping He hears their woes
Of penance in a sinful cadence.
How can God hear such repentance?
It's not incompetence-
It's his transcendence!
God has no ears or eyes
To despise or praise
To hear those woes and see those tears.
A sentient world He is not
A causal world He does not plot,
He'd not be God if he was of a fleshly lot.
Hope and pray all you will,
The God you want is silent and still.
It matters not how loud you yell,
He is nothing more than a spell-
Created to avoid hell.
Transcendence puts the mind to rest.
Every prayer unheard –
An echo in a transient world
He can't attend-
He's not a transitory Thing-
He's a transcendent Thing.

This takes the nod
And ties the sceptic's knot.
Beliefs are hollow things.
They slay reason and tame the brain-
Make them beacons for shame.
Nothing can be said
When God exceeds our grasp.
No partnership exists
No love persists
Only the rift
Of ignorant men
Who believe
In a broken scheme.

Fire and shadows

Fire and shadows - companions for millenniums,
dancing together in caves, on cabin walls,
across floors and ceilings in endless harmony.
Stirring Christians to servile conformity
Unsettling pagans to seek tranquility.
Fire and shadows - companions for millenniums,
dancing together in caves, on cabin walls,
across floors and ceilings in endless harmony.
Stirring Christians to servile conformity
Unsettling pagans to seek tranquility.

Kumba the Native Boy

Kumba was a native boy
Never shipped ahoy
Never traveled far and saw a foreign land
Never had a Bible in his hand
Knew nothing of the Redeemer – before his time.
But Kumba had a vision
And created a new religion -
Called it Christianity
And claimed candidly
he saw a man upon a cross
Called him Jesus the redeemer
Saw his suffering demeanor
And began to shun his pagan leader
And Declare Him King of Men and Son of God
And built a church to worship his new found Friend;
Converted other natives to cease their heathen ends,
And blessed them like an apostle
And begged them to mend their primitive ways
And worship and give praise
To a portrait of the new Redeemer on a crucifix -
Contrived of consecrated sticks -
Above an altar made of stones and planks
That after they began to genuflect
They were transfixed.

Soon it came to him
As they were singing a hymn
That Baptism freed them of sin.
He directed them to Lake Unin
And baptized the minion
Exclaiming that if we met with extinction
God would make no distinction
Our souls would ascend to heaven without restriction.

Ten commandments, an inspiration, came to him a dream –
They gained esteem,
Became part of his saintly scheme
The native clan surrendered their pagan ways
Adopted their Christian faith to the end of their days.
The tribe thought him a saintly man
declared him a helmsman

And a prophet and a priestly clergyman of the land.
The clan attended church on Sunday morning -
Not a parishioner could be seen yawning
When he preached the gospels –
They came to him in a vision like an apostle.
They began to confide in him and confess their sins
Take Holy Communion for the sake of their Savior – their spiritual kin.
They accepted his blessings with a joyful grin
Now they have been saved and free of sin.
Righteous, he remained, all the days of his life,
Created a new religion –
Called himself a Christian.
No priest or pastor attempted an immersion,
Or a missionary attempted a conversion.
It was a vision of his own excursion
That claimed his Christian soul.
When he wasn't preaching
And exorcising sinners with his teaching
Spent his time on rocky streets
Blessing trinkets for his Lord
And proffering them to the poor.
Converting every whore -
And prayed for their deliverance so they'd sin no more.
Allegiance they swore,
And promised to tend to the poor.
He was a saintly man, who thought it best, to save mankind.
He began to blessed himself all the time
And uttered "Father, Son, Holy Ghost" –
An urge that came to him when he was disposed
To seek heaven and praise the Lord for this rightful celebration.
His cross fashioned from heart wood,
Remained affixed above an altar where he stood
In his lowly frock and hood
He planted the sacred host
On each parishioner's tongue -
Their spirit over-come.
For years he spread the Word
His parishioners were so stirred
No one dared to expunge
A vision so fecund.

Their pagan life was abolished.
His Christian pilgrimage embellished

The village was blessed and replenished
Suddenly his life and his Christian faith vanished
Kumba the saintly man died in his sleep one wintry night
His soul took flight to a heavenly light
Abandoning his earthly appetites
To face judgment day -
Not expecting to be betrayed.
Instead he was decreed a heathen still,
His religion a deluded spell.
A heathen must be converted first
Otherwise he's cursed –
Can't have a vision of his own
He's not a Jew or an Anglo Saxon.
"You weren't ordained by a priest,
"Hell is where you belong - you counterfeit"
"You weren't anointed by a pastor in scared robes, ordained by God."
"No one declared you a righteous Christian and converted you to the fold."
"Only an ordained man and his rightful flock can lay claim to heaven
And declare themselves a Christian"
"Your vision is a sham."
"God would declare it a scam -
"A simple native could not have Christian plan",
A sanctimonious voice concluded.
Kumba was cast in hell for his vision of a Christian life -
Pretending to invent the Christian religion brought nothing but strife
His vision wasn't ordained by God- they had to be denied
He couldn't live a righteous life,
Converting natives to forfeit their pagan strife.
Simple and devout – yet Christians had their doubt -
Proclaimed against his fame with a shameful flout.
Chagrined by their intemperate clout
And their insistent doubt
His piety at stake,
He recited biblical passages to show he wasn't a fake
How would he know such things?
If he never had a Bible to show such a whim
Even then he was still a primitive cretin -
His guileless humility forsaken
Heaven's gate was closed to him
His evangelical dream another whim
The light of paradise dimmed.
All conversions from pagan to religion
Weren't worth a smidgen –

Thought to be null and void
Christians must avoid.
Now that he was told
He had no place in heaven to hold
And came eye to eye with the awful truth
And peered into this heartless and indignant abuse
When the door of paradise was slammed in his face.
Who ordained the priests, blessed the robes in ornate lace?
Declared what was divine in the first place?
What is wrong with a simple native unrefined,
Granted an unbidden vision to create a religion sorely defined.
How does anyone know Kumba wasn't part of His design?
Or knows that he was denied a self-righteous plan?
And dismissed his legion of converted fans?
Who can declare a preordained monopoly? –
Hording a prescription to begin a religion?
Deprived poor Kumba his rightful collusion?
Joseph Smith began a religion
With polygamy permitted and he's forgiven.
Claimed Jesus resurrected again
And told the Mormons don't abstain
Take as many virgins as you can claim.
No one points with a finger of shame.
Or claims that they are inane
To say Jesus dropped from heaven and walked the plains -
Watched them usher their virgins to Utah.
Who has the right to make the divine call?
Smith?
Luther?
Kumba took no virgins hostage,
Believed in the scripture,
Caused no fuss over the eucharist,
Wasn't an antisemitic,
Didn't start a war - slandering peasants,
And was the least inclined
To start a free-for-all over the divine.
He gripped his hand-made rosary
Felt his tumescent heart in misery
Walked down perdition's path,
Felt the heat of Hades' wrath
Began to relinquish the dream he had -
Wondering why he wasn't included in those braggart's plan?

Shadow of Love

Lost Love

Your eyes beckoned me
And I stumbled into your soul-willingly
Right into the middle of it.
I looked hither and thither-nothing to gain;
It was all the same:
An azure sea cast in a blazing golden flame.
But to my surprise
The crest of a wave did rise-
A reprise I thought;
A faint image arose
Like a memory of long ago
Of a sandy beach in sunlight all aglow,
And a gale did follow and grab me like an aerotow
And guide me forlorn and alone
On uncharted waves
To an unknown land -
An outcast marooned
And forsworn to atone
A self-declaration of my own
For a love that was never sewn
A love that was never known.
An eternal scar that marked
The bones of our destiny.

I rest upon this shore of loneliness
Time like an arrow pierces my heart
The aloofness I feel I can't scale.
What we lost will prevail.
My solitude is like a veil
That covers my travail.
The moment was pregnant with desire -
Lips were pressed with fire
It was imminent this sensuous flair
A moment we would be devoured -
An inundating bliss lost in the mist
To that voice echoing the same animus
Reminding me it wasn't to be - this moment so glorious!
A luminous memory that would never prevail
A moment restrained
Never to ordained
Never to be reminisced.

Instead, came the whisper
"No. No. We can't be pressed
To pluck the day and be led astray
Ensnared by the Satyr fire.
We can't let the deed transpire!"

"It's your beauty I want to touch
Your soul is not enough
To quell this sensuous rush.
I followed you - a beloved pawn
In a sea of love
With amorphous maps
Vaguely drawn
As the waves of passion
Tossed us back and forth
Between heaven and earth
Until we gave that moment birth."

Carpe diem brought a torrid tide
Passion and love codified.
Afraid the seed would not be denied
She declined.
The moment withered on the vine
Stolen like a cutpurse -
Satyr's curse?
Bliss lost in time
Caught in a bind
As if was a crime?
Risks that blind?
The decree was unrefined?
A warning to unwind?
No longer a love to be entwined
The apex of love denied.
Let this summer memory flounder -
Nothing left to ponder
Of a love forsaken its ardor.

Vortex of Love and Death

Bury yourself in this love
Do not be deterred by this neoteric cusp
Torn asunder by golden tipped flames of death
That ripped flesh and bones with ease and zest.
Quenched by floating canisters of SC gas seeking a breathless quest
Bobbed and bounced on the commons and up the little crest of death
Burned the eyes and seared the lungs and quieted the chest.
Blood spewed out like spring fountains on the sanguine crest.
The timid Maple buds opened their little wombs to begin their quest-
Heeding the sun's request.
Writhing bodies in the throes of death above their roots
As the bell rang its final clarion ring of distress.
My lover's hand did touch the stream of blood she confessed.
Hot and thick like lava she said
After the sound of M-1's echoed through the town unblessed.

Did we deserve this love so mightily felt?
Where heaven dwelt
And the soul unsealed the secrets in a weald.
We are history's children born of pain and blood
Our peers were gassed and left for dead
In a field filled with dread.
Metal bears our scars and does not bleed
A stark reminder of the deed.
Come my love with that blood drenched hand
To this vortex of peace where are souls are healed
In the flame of love and we are united as one.
Death calls to us one day and our love and what we have won
And the riddled bodies of our dying peers and what was done
Will be seared on the grassy knoll in sunlight
And the voices of the dead will cry out in the night.
Deeds done on that day shattered our love
Our naked arms thrashing in misty bromide
That burned our lips and eyes.
from our mouth on our naked lips
We consummated our love
In that town on where we were one
On the field of death and blood.
That scared our souls.

I Will Sleep in Her Soul

To Deborah

I will sleep in her soul,
Be content that it will console
The forlorn yearning lost long ago
That had a worthy zest
That I had to put to rest
And the love that I did quest
That was buried
In a silent grave -
A lost memory,
That resurrects in a reverie
And unnerves my serenity.

This urge I cannot quell
And the voice that continues to dwell
Reminds me of the death knell
That long ago I had to bid farewell
To a love that spun me into a spell
But beckons me still -
"Stir up her womb
Just once.
Make it shutter
With delight-
Go on -
Enrich your life;
Have its delight -
In the sensual night."

The dream was lost long ago
I must be content to sleep in her soul
And forgo all hopes of those tantalizing sights
And carnal heights
Convince myself it's best
To cede to a sacrificial test
And let those passions rest.

But, again, I am beset
By the voice that that will not let me rest
That reminds of this everlasting debt
When my love and I met.

And we were forced to forget
The amorous bliss we'd beget.
As long as my bones are wrapped in flesh
This lost consummation still haunts me afresh
And the voice will not rest
It lets me relive this lost quest
"Go on" it will profess
"You wanted so much
To touch her flesh -
To beg her to yield and confess
And not digress
From those passions of the breast.
"Try once again to transgress.
Let us coalesce –
Feel the passion we possess."

I could settle
To have plucked one little petal -
From love's delicate portal
And cherished that moment -
More than the sound of an angel's trumpet -
And left me breathless -
In that sensuous cleft
And the blue orchid on her breast –
Even if it remained unrequited
I had that one dream
Of an erotic beguine -
Just one dance
Breath to breath
Unstable lips that barely greet
Desperately trying to meet
But will not admit defeat,
They still entreat
Sacrificed to the loins
That never lie! -
They know
The rhythm of life
Without strife
And may keep the lips apart -
A most fair sacrifice
And that will suffice
For those brief undulating moments in Paradise.

Again, I'll close the door
And relinquish the seed
Of hope for the passionate deed
That bore the flame
And not hold us to blame
For abstaining from love's flame -
A coup de main -
That forced us to abstain
Feared the womb
Would be filled with more than love's flame.

The fantasy still remains
The consummation in a dream
The heart rife with joy
The senses - no ploy.
The racing pulse rejoicing.
The everlasting zest still feasting
In my soul –
Taking its heartfelt toll.

I can't silence that persistent yearning in my breast
And mute that voice at its tempestuous crest
As it cries out at night
To seek again
That sensuous spark
That's unafraid to part
The petals of the wild orchid
And feel the foxgloves fire in her heart,
Quiet like a hummingbird hovering over her
I'd undulate soft and slow
Until we had an amorous glow
Savoring the moment in a quiet thrill
Slowly still
Eye to eye-
Each like a harmless spy
Taking a chance
To steal one eternal glance
Into our souls - a beloved trance, at last!
And in the fleshly robe perchance
We'd let passion commence
In the room full of love and frankincense.

This idle dream must cease
That union and the irreverent swooning appeased.
I must pin
That dream
Upon the stream of time
Leave it
And disembark
Into the dark
Of an unfamiliar land
And sleep forever in her soul.

And never more
Shall I implore
This lost love of yesteryear
That makes me demand
Her hand
Clinched in mine -
Delicate and refined,
Dreaming that she's trembling
Unafraid of the rendering sweat
The hard twists and deep thrusts
When pleasure doth rise
With a pulsing surprise -
That brief potent
Transcendent moment
A gift of the flesh
That could redress
A love that was unblessed –
Never acquiesced.

But I've deceived myself long enough
Let that fantasy be undone -
But only when I sleep in the dusty earth
Or in the ashes of an urn
Will I cease to yearn
For that naked moment in the sun
When you were mine
In that glare of time,
Lost in the rhyme
of each breathless thrust
Like a little tempest
That would sustain her trust
And we'd be reborn

To the sound of a lover's storm.
Stillborn was this love
Never to be sanctified with an earthly thrust
Or a breathless brush
Upon the lips at dusk.
I must be content to sleep in your soul
For the robust day is gone never to unfold
An unrequited love to behold
A lost memory that had been sold
To an eclipse in time-innocently foiled.
I can pretend
To relish this unconsummated end -
Close my eyes and ascend
To the sublime and transcend -
Avert the fleshly trend.
But the dream resumes instead
To turn those sullen lips rosy red
Resume the quest -
Force the moment back to a naked dusk.
But that course is denied;
I must concede
To forfeit that dream
Only the dust can purge
And stick to a fleshless illusion
Until the winds of eternity
Brush across my face,
Resigned, once again, to sleep in your soul.

Lovers' Enigma

Wrap me in your arms of death
until we take our final breath.
A cocoon of sheets and blankets envelop us like a makeshift womb,
and bundles us against our worldly wounds.
We entwine ourselves with legs and arms -
our bones and skin, once the pleasure of peccant felicity and sin,
are now a reprieve that reenacts our end.
We twist and turn in a lively chase
in our nightly flight to find that one impossible place
wherein we can settle in a peaceful embrace -
one halting breath from death.
You press your hands together like a supplicant in prayer,
slide them against your cheek and rest your head upon our liar –
and bid fair-well and await the sleepy stare.
We repose once again in our cozy bliss -
mocking and mimicking death.
Your drifting hair caresses my skin,
I notice again your sensuous grin.
In our restless sleep -
the covers in a wavy heap
like the ebb and flow of the tide on a sandy beach -
We hatch our silent dreams no one can breech
in sleep's repose no can reach
like those entombed in a crypt long ago.
A twitch or a moan
brings us back and we quickly retain our earthly pose.
We journey back from this foreign land
we neither know or understand.
I gently squeeze her to see if she was swept away -
Was spared for another day.

Each morning we rise to another birth;
each night we retire to another death -
If we rise and pass the test,
we know it's a rehearsal for our final rest.
A feather to a lip opines a playful awakening,
and we greet each other without a hint of wavering.
We rise to the morning sun
one more resurrection before our final run.
Grateful to be ravening lovers at play -
Sworn to keep that final breath away.

Embrace each other's flesh again -
a passionate display without refrain
audible gasps unrestrained
until the pinnacle reigned.

One more night together we silently implore
before time sends us packing to a breathless shore.
Nothing on earth can stay intact.
But lovers always ask:
Aren't we more than a wayward task -
Won't our flights see their way toward heaven's light? -
send us hurling beyond an earthly chart?
Our transcendent trysts
Immortal in our merging thrusts?
Is it all for not - an empty cup? -
When our bodies gave us the slip
And death sent us on our final trip
Will our bones be the only witness to our passionate script?

A Lover's Lamentation

There upon the bed
She used to lie.
The little cradle,
Upon the pillow -
Where her sleepy head - abandoned long ago -
Was left untouched
Like an artist's mold -
Unfinished - awaiting the fire and kiln
Reminded him of their love - half born -
When he clutched
And pressed upon her breasts
With that relentless haste,
Never giving her thighs a rest.
Her soul in all this ingress
Was ignored
Tossed aside -
Abandoned
Like an empty shell.

At times, they were like shadows
On the wall
Their love so hollow
Never once did he allow
His eyes to follow
That inward glance
And take that chance
To follow love's path.
He was bemused
And failed to see the golden light of the muse
Or consummate it in the sensual flame
Without remorse or shame.
Her love he did shun,
In the penumbra of a celestial sun.
Even when his heart skipped a beat
In that swirling sensual heat
He fell, effete
in the eclipse of defeat.

Memories like reflections in a mirror
Bringing our past ever nearer
Reminding us of lost splendor,

And those wounds of yesteryear.
Like an arrow in a bow
Growing tighter until a vow
Pricks the conscience of a lonely soul.
And the restless urge to extol
The maiden he failed to behold
In those nocturnal delights
That filled their nights.
Suddenly in a trance
He saw her in mist
A vision he couldn't resist.
Time ceased to exist
As in an angel's dream.
Her specter brought him shame.
Her bright eyes like blazing flames
Her skin fair with an amber glow
Her thick hair curled, twisted and flowed
In dangling dark arcs
Down her shoulders – quite stark
In contrast to the rosy mist
Rising up and around her thighs and waist
Cast an image of beauty - both sublime and sensuous.
He wished she were here
Once again
To give him one more chance,
To have one more glance,
To have one more turn
And see the hollow shape return -
Fill the pillow with her locks and curls -
And hear the purls
Of yesteryear.
Perhaps he would peer into her eyes
And see the blazing flame of ecstasy
And the supernal love of the sublime,
And let them intermingle without enmity -
Between a breathless union
And a muse of resolution.
To see she was the muse of emerald and gold -
The goddess of an unbridled rapture
He failed to capture.

Shadows and Light – Lovers Delight

Shadows and light - lovers delight
They squander not their conjugal embrace
Take carnal delight in that intricate place
Intricately locked arm in arm in that intimate pace ,
Like shadows and light intermingling in their intimate display
Like lovers, they mix and match in space,
Never fixed in place.
When a shadow moves,
Does it intrude
And the light is fixed?
Or when the light moves
Does it intrude
And the shadow is fixed?
Or are they rude and intermix?
It's hard to say –
Perhaps they shift as one
As lovers do?
Tricking the eye in disgrace.
Both together a phantasmagoria makes
To delight the senses in a mystical play.
Moonlight and shadows may abide the secrets of lovers,
Reveal nothing of their passionate embraces,
Or love's rapture-their whispering moans and heedless caresses,
Their heated breaths and panting sighs and secret confessions -
Gossip free and held in trust by those shadows and light
As they are contrite to intermingle throughout the night.

Light and shadow have always been about
Even before those lovers conceded to those sensual bouts
If they had memories to titillate
They'd reveal in those myriads of nights
The screams of labor and the cries of birth.
Tales would abound in the munificent flames of life and death
And the opaque landscape of night and shadows -
Twisting and wrenching secrets on wintry nights
From the heart of darkness and the song of light.

Death Is Never Remiss

Death

Friend or foe I do not know.
Like a lover or a kin
I think of you without end.
In the shadow of time -
I have met you often
saw your bleak and inimical presence in coffins
on gurneys and hospital beds
when your victims ceased tossing
and lay supine in a breathless resign
left in their twisted and wrinkled sheets
With that frozen stare – that final retreat -
and that peculiar look of surprise and despair –
stark and austere -
before the sheets were straightened and tossed in the air
to cover the face after their frightful affair
and their final solitaire prayer.
You cease all suffering and pain,
after you have put in your bid and claim.
But what price there is to pay for such a gain!

Some appreciate your helping hand -
willing to give in and stop making a stand,
and greet you like a gentle friend -
a Godsend that brings about your end:
"Take me! I cannot mend!"
come the plaintive words of a dying man.
Sometimes you're given a helping hand,
murder or suicide renders aid to your resolute plan -
those helpful bystanders that can shorten a lifespan.

Fearful ones refuse your command
and carry on as planned,
continue to wince and grovel and bargain in pain -
"spare me", they declare, once again -
fearful of your ultimate demand.
They'd rather suffer another day
and cling to their malady
until you become weary and swats them away.

Sometimes you're slick
And make it quick -

an unexpected twinge in the chest,
one short breath,
and, brusquely, the poor fool is laid to rest -
not much of a surprise,
no way to lay claim to another sunrise.
You can be kind, it seems -
appear in an elderly woman's dreams
and sweep her off her feet
while she sleeps.
You never disappoint – pledged to fate.
you always keep your date.

You can be like a blind date -
a surprise before the open gate.
Sometimes you're like an insufferably boring date -
until they take your bait
and you step in and render them a rebate.
Many linger for hours, even days, before you intercede
and remove their distress
without the slightest redress.
We can't speak ill of you,
you didn't deliberate the means of our fate –
you only stole our breath -
stepped in to end our strife.
You had nothing to do with Demeter's loss or Persephone's fate,
or coaxed us to celebrate in any way our fate
or give us any reason to participate -
in October - the Eleusinian Mysteries' date -
in the ritualistic cycle of life and death
in the Hall of Initiation by flickering torchlight,
dancing and chanting and feeling contrite
with exulted delight.

You aren't so tranquil or kind
or in need of celebration –
you are embedded in creation
to further our suffering and vexation.
You may end our life sooner than we like
but not for spite -
you don't care if we are a neophyte
or a decrepit man who stumbles in the moonlight -
you're on call at all times
show no partiality

and step in when necessary.
You may curtail the ending of our life
and we are left to curb our pain and fright -
ready or not It comes with your own peculiar delight.

Any notion of an afterlife
needs to be maligned.
Purging sins for being unkind
praying to God to be redeemed
repudiating the sins of mankind
even when exulting libations of joy, we expend
for God's assured love that will yield
Heaven's blessings unconcealed
are all nothing more than a penitent's drunken binge -
an illusion that came unhinged.
There's no redemption
heaven or bliss
just an eternal nothingness.
God is like a knot that can't be untied
His fictitious presence is known far and wide.

Other myths have charming twists
fondly lacking in verity
and must be dismissed:
Some believe we're offered a reprieve
in another mythical scheme,
but Thanatos was tricked by shrewd Sisyphus
to avoid a stint in Tartarus.
"Show me how these chains do work", Sisyphus declared;
Thanatos complied and chained himself to a rock –
what a cunning plot
to cheat death –
to outdo this inexorable fate -
sparing the demise of mortals,
encumbered by Sisyphus' smiles.
Thanatos was unchained and tricked no more
sends the unwilling victims to the morgue.
Myths are airy portraits of deities and demigods,
and speak of nature amiss,
but truth is never on their list
or spoken by a demigod's lips -
those natural laws that chain us all
are beyond their grasp,

and make us gasp
when death is at hand.
They can't understand
personifying death as an unkind friend
or a vicious fiend
or a celebrated fan
for a transcendent plan
needs to be banned.

We must not be immured
by such shenanigans.
Death is nothing but what has to be inured
as our life comes to a close
like the winter snow that buries a rockrose.
Death rids the world of suffering -
It's a common thread
but renders an empty silence in its stead.
It can't be explained by myth or religious fervor -
nothing appeases its fearful clutches
or explains away why there is so much despair and suffering.
Whatever opened the sadistic gate
that only death can abate
is a mystery beyond debate.
Friend or foe we do not know,
until the moment grows,
but the fear we feel redoubles
with each passing year.
God is not the architect of our fate,
commands the bid for death's date.
There is no auctioneer for our fate -
only an unknown legacy of eternal silence
a shadow eclipsing a budding iris.
Our bones and the dust upon the plains
are all that remains
and all that we can claim.
The bridge of time and the memories we have,
joins the living with the dead.

Gravesites Are Popular Places

Gravesites are popular places-
Hangouts for all ages and races.
A child finds solace here
After a bout with diphtheria
A mother, too, when child-birth became too much to bare -
Their infants cry was never heard after the agonizing affair.
Death ends our despair
The last breath of despondency is released into the air
Our last groan is seen with a sympathetic stare.
The earth becomes a well-made bed
for the bones of the dead.
No more languishing or suffering,
Covers for shuffling,
Complaints of suffering,
Sympathetic muttering.

Visitors soon learn
Not to yearn
For the deceased to apprehend -
Their prayers are in the summer wind - their only friend.
Those love ones long departed
May be true-hearted
But aloof, a bit standoffish and decisively introverted.
Even though they never boost
It soon becomes obvious they are a bad host,
But the love that's never lost
Remains a silent loyalty -
Prayers may reach the dead ears of fealty
May be lost in transiency.
The dead always retain, with unflagging tenacity,
A smug aristocracy.
But their ceaseless cold shoulder
And their relentless reticence to the beholder
Didn't curtail those graveside bystanders
To hope for an eternal vigilance
And a fellowship of silence.
Companions of the soil
Children who will never stroll
Upon the earth - hand upon the scroll
Of the sunlight and shadows of life's toil.
And sustains the ruse of talking to the dead

The seasons come and go; they remain resolute in their dreamless pauses-
A rigorous silence only the dead have perfected without reticence.
The very old are fleshless- nothing left but bits of bones.
Some, however, are still dressed in their Sunday best,
Posing in their silent way like they had another day:
Their suits are neatly pressed; their ties cinched tightly around their necks,
Dresses are neatly tucked with little pastel roses that will never be plucked.
Years, after the tears have dried,
Callers continue with adoration and pain to fall for their ruse-
Trying to please the departed, thinking they are taking a snooze.
Some stand over their earthly bed talking to them as if they can be revived -
"Saw your brother yesterday. He's still alive."
"Didn't have much to say. Says he'll come by and stay awhile"
"Might come and see you in the fall."
"Wants the corn husked and hauled."
Another might be heard to say
"Miss ya, Ellie May. Went to our class reunion yesterday."
"Remember Fred? He didn't know you were dead."
Some grave yard chats are more like left over spats:
"Why did you take such a risk? Now you're nothing but dust."
Others speak of a reunion after their demise, pointing to the skies:
"It'll be a pleasant surprise to see Eddie Grimes. Like old times."
"I miss you Mary dear, I swear. Can't wait to hold you in my arms."
"Still have my same wit and charms."
Heaven never hears these plaintive moans or comforting tones;
It's only sky that claims these plaintive groans
That's as far as it goes - muted when the wind blows.
Time and death are accomplices in the same conspiracy
Silence is the bond – death's tyranny-
The living are forced to agree upon.
Dust is all that carries on after we are gone.
Heaven's gate, the illusive bait, obfuscates the truth:
There is no afterlife to comfort or soothe;
Just a mirthless hope that sustains the ruse
And helps us cope.

Graves are good for tidying-up, leaving fresh roses,
And leaving for a sullen road
With jumbled memories of long ago
A fearful munificence of the dead.

Summer Dare

Lie on a grave like a bed,
Tombstone at your head
With the name of the dead
And stretch out on a summer eve
And feel the warm summer breeze
Brush against your skin with ease.
Stare up at the night sky
And watch a star blink -
A beckoning wink.
Are these the eyes of the departed
In a land no one has chartered
On their deathwatch
Seeking refuge in a loved one's heart?

Each Breath

Each breath is like a saber
Lancing at death.
A battle that can't be won
No matter how well spun.
But another breath
Postpones the scythe -
One more day off the hook
One more day to defend our earthly nook -
One more reprieve death can't rook.

Go on and seek the Golden Hive
And the nectar of Love.
It begins with the flesh
That gives it a shove
Toward an unwarranted love,
But not for confines above -
Or the hordes caprice,
But for the silent peace
Where the bones and soul rest
And there is no need to be blest
Or pass a test.
Love is the only gateway to heaven
Sin and degradation are for pastors and pests.
Like all the rest they had one chance
To gloat at a being a divine guest.
Most are forgotten
In their silent dismay and disappointment.
They're filled with discontent
Over their dissolution
If they could rise and see
Their decree was not a solution.
Their resting bones without resolution
And their spirit and its deeds have no zest
Left behind with their earthly rest,
Suited for those glebe guests.
The lover's quest
Or the poets rhyming text
Are all that passes the immortality test.

The Deepest Sleep

Death is the deepest sleep of all,
No tossing or turning, twisting or rolling
No unruly snoring to disturb the peace
No alarm clock to buzz and bring about a fuss
No bed to make, sheets to wash or fold
No ashtrays to empty or lights to turn off.
No dreams to frighten or write about
No aches or pains to complain about -
No stiff limbs, muscle cramps, or a sore back to scoff about
No restless thoughts to unsettle the mind –
Just an eternal dreamless sleep in oblivion's eye.
"Do not Disturb" is written in the sky -
No roster to descry
Just a tombstone no one can deny.

The Party

Everyone is invited
Not a soul is slighted
Expect a summons -
This party has no shortcomings.
Some believe the host is divine;
Others believe there is no heavenly design.
Whether or not there is a sponsor,
An invitation is never squandered.
Some resent being invited;
Others are relieved and grateful when entreated.
A few never know they were solicited.
An invitation so brisk and definitive;
Nevertheless, no one is blighted.

Some are summoned in their sleep;
Some give in after a painful retreat.
Others clamor for their own receipt -
Take it upon themselves to set their own date.
Some beg for an insufferable bidding –
Feel deprived when they are left suffering,
Lingering far too long waiting for their invitation.
Some resist the party
Other don't want to be tardy.
Old or young
White or black
Oriental or Italian
It makes no matter –
Favoritism never matters;
The party is all the same for every captor -
Races sing the same song –
They all belong!

Some invitations arrive after pneumonia.
An infant gets one with progeria or diphtheria.
Others find their invitation after Huntington's disease –
An invitation gladly received,
Especially, if it's CRPS or the "suicide disease".
Tsunamis hand out many solicitations,
Swooping up many with quick and foreordained ovations -
Those certain and quick invitations.
Nature's fearless fury

Sends many to the party.
Plagues bring partygoers in droves
A celerity of invitations for myriads of souls.
No one is ever left out
Especially after painful bouts
Of urate crystals circulating about -
Nothing like a good round of gout!
FOP is and instant hit
Any partygoer will readily admit -
Stiffen up and give one last sigh,
As any merrymaker will testify.
Those who aren't yet to attend
Fate will gladly portend
An invitation that will soon amend
Any exclusion that might offend -
Soon a breathless fate awaits
A date is set to meet those party mates.
Merry makers for perpetuity -
A timeless constancy.
No hangovers or inebriated fools,
Who brag or tell another ruse.
No dancing or loud music -
Or the popping of floating balloons,
Or squeaking of party horns,
Or the vanquishing of evil - smashing the pinata.
Just a silent retreat -
Where everyone is perennially discreet.

Skin and Bones

What keeps the skin taunt against the bones?
Keeps it stretching over the years?
Yet there are no tears
When the bones are pressed
And seem to break.
I can only extrapolate
How the skin holds its place
Like the woman with her lace -
Snapping without shame or disgrace -
Nimbly pulling and tugging and the stocking does not tear
As its drawn taunt against her leg without fear.
The bones aren't pinched or crushed - only cinched.
Worn snugly beneath the skin.
Years of pressing and fondling
To no avail – it holds its shape with all that jostling -
Steadfast in its prime.

And what makes it droop and sag?
Like an old sackcloth or an overused rag
That's out lived its time.
The frail bones relieved of their grind
No longer press against the skin's erstwhile bind.
The bones surrender
The skin can't remember -
Slaves to time
And the wrinkles of a crime
That portentous sign of our imminent demise.

Bird at the Window

A small bird flips and flops against a window pane,
it can't abstain,
its refuses to see its tenacious efforts are in vain-
space with wafting air must be there.
Tricked by the illusion of transparency
it bangs and thumps in spurts until it's maimed and hurts-
Neither exhaustion or threat of death averts!
Why does it bank on a losing bet?
No cosmic conspiracy compels it to toil and sweat-
Space with wafting air must be there.

If it only had the tack to discern
180 degrees of salvation at its back.
If it only had the tack
to relinquish its suicidal tenacity to attack
and give the window pane some slack,
but its preset doom is a snap.
It's not the enemy that's bending its beak and breaking its back.
Put an end to this little din- redeem yourself and fly a different track-
No intervention will preserve your death.
Cease this mission of despair, confusing a transparent pane for air-
It's not your ally or friend;
it's a snare to pin you in,
nothing to portend- but your end.
"Thump" "Thump"
"Thump" "Thump"
"Thump" "Thump"
The death knell of defeat
a primitive drumbeat of pain and retreat.
Does nature smile at this mockery of instinct?
Knowing it can't adapt
and find its way out of this lethal trap?
As long as those wings flap
And the window's transparency offers no escape
And the ceaseless urge is fortified
And a blindness to its doom is certified,
Nature's foolish trap is set.
What's the point of such a decree-?
This hypnotic esprit,
This orgy of rhythmic pain
This senseless bartering with a didactic window pane.

Is this transitory gloom a metaphor for our doom?
A foreboding contingency portending our end
like the transparent illusion of the window pane?
An elixir sniffed through the nose
or injected in a vein to keep us from our woes
we lack a will to oppose.
Beguiled like the bird-
banking on transparency
and its unrelenting temptation
to fly through window pane
and be excised by the skies-
we prick holes in our veins
for that illusionary peace of mind.
And lose our will in the maze
of hallucinations that make us slaves.
The bird's useless fluttering against the window pane
Its perennial enterprise of pain
like the overtures of an unrequited lover-
indefatigably vain.
Is he a blundering fool?
Sainthood in disguise?
It's an untiring deed
An implacable commission-
Like a bird's relentless collision-
His rebuffed hand of a hopeless lover.

Time is the window pane of bird and man?
The gamesman of their span
The helmsman of their destiny
without clemency.
They both flutter an ordained feat
That always ends in defeat.
They never feel the plunging pain
of this window pane
until the end- deceived by its absence
and its ill-regarded sanctions.

We traverse the span
Like a plow in a barren land
Hoping time will yield
Another day on sunny field
in a lover's arms.

We don't hear those silent alarms
Until the stealth of death steals our breath
and we lie in our bed-
dead-
with sheets over our head.

Locus Amoenus

A festive retreat
Where song and dance keep a steady beat
In the stately Locus Amoenus,
For rebellious, pleasure- seeking, youths.
A spectacle to behold, especially at night
When those bright red and yellow florescent lights
Set off its rather garish décor
Where lovers can explore.
This flashy hideaway stands on a bluff – proud and high
A palace overlooking a mighty river passing by
Calm and quiet in the summer,
Rife with stormy moods in the winter,
Etched before breath was taken -
Primitive, measureless, eternally awakened.
Through those windows below a blue sky
Large maples and weeping willows catch the eye.
As summer orchards decked in blossoms cause a sigh.
Branches are filled with chirping robins in July,
After Winter mountains are no longer snow bound,
And wolves roamed and howled -
Yearning for spring,
As the town shrugged off a winter's chagrin
With a joyous grin.
Those breathless views are shunned
By lovers who succumb
To the dreams in those records that spun
Those lyrics of love,
Especially when "You Send Me" rocks
From the garish jute box
Castings its magic spell
Where love can't be dispelled
In the pleasure palace,
Where a nickel or two filled it with life -
The silver slot when running hot,
Kept it humming with golden tunes
Of rock and roll
From Chuck Berry to Fats Domino.
"Maybellene" and "Ain't That a Shame"
Resonates with soulful acclaim.
"Rock Around the Clock"
A heavy beat with a crooning melody from The Comets.

Melodies from "Only You" and "Twilight Time"
Float on waves of hope and desire,
Casting spells on all that lovers admire.
Silent interludes, like an annoying guest,
Stir up barbaric howls and irascible yelps
Until the unkind silent interloper left:
A nickel soon boots the pest from Locus Amoenus,
As The Temptations' "Earth Angel", and "My Girl"
Fill the dreams in a lover's whirl,
As sweaty, perfumed bodies jump off long legged stools,
And spin and swirl around the dance floor.

When winter breathed cold winds into the valleys,
When the sun lost its way more quickly in the mountains,
Hovering below frozen cliffs,
And hidden rifts,
As evenings brought shadows
As the crepuscular haze of night arose,
lovers in the Locus Amoenus were predisposed
To those musical tones
Of spinning records
And slurping down sodas,
Perked up the dull and dreary days of the winter.
Teens in the twilight seek the Alcazar,
Filling it with joyful chatter.
The ornate jukebox –
With its flashy green chrome glass tubes –
Just a nickel plays those tunes
That quells any lover's feud.
Slipping a coin into a gaping silver slot,
Titillates the flashy music box,
When a "45" drops on a revolving platter -
A blissful merger with a needle and a record.
When a finger presses "B-12",
Presley's "Love Me" or "Jailhouse Rock" casts a spell
That foretells where lovers dwell
When his mellifluous voice compels
Those lovers to rebel.
When "C-13" is pressed,
A lover's heart is blessed
With the jivey "Whole lotta love" -
Its rhythm and lyrics make a lover's face blush.
"A-10" plays "Earth Angel", as those dancers flush.

"F-6" plays the forlorn lover's delight - "Runaway" -
Appeals to those who are cavalier and risqué.
Those incarnated voices – a sensuous ploy -
From the numerous vinyl "45's" of joy -
Were performed on the snazzy Seeburg -
Thinking it's a concert,
Those lovers become alert.
Buddy Holly's tenor
And Roy Orbison's baritone
Or Johnny Cash's base
Are piped out in a flash.
The Jerry Allison's drums accompanied "Peggy Sue"
As Baker's guitar makes its debut, -
Strumming out "love is Strange".
Lee Allen's saxophone accompanies Little Richard
And Jerry Lee Lewis's piano pounds out notes like a blizzard,
As lovers twist and turn in bliss.

The Locus Amoenus is like an oasis,
A cult of Bacchus - sensuous and rapacious
A world apart, hot, active, free of constraints,
A palace where memories of love prevailed,
A heart frames initials carved on table tops -
Lover's prompts –
Etched with a knife -
As "Pretty Woman" plays like a lover in strife.
It is a place for a lover's quest
Where dreams unfold
And memories – behold! -
Etched on souls that are never consoled.
Another sullen lover plays "Runaway",
And watches with forlorn gaze
The sacred river pass by,
Wandering, ocean bound,
With a mazy motion toward a blissful embrace -
Tumbling, tumultuous, with erratic grace,
As another record hits the groove with haste
And "All I have to Do is Dream" listlessly plays
After another "45" falls in place.

Another Dawn

Each breath is a skirmish with death
Many in a day is a war won
Another day in the sun.
Another day the invitation to the party that did not come.   -
A reprieve from the worms' relentless feast -
A savagery worse than any beast.

So, go on and seek the Golden Hive
And the nectar of Love.
It begins with the flesh
With lovers possessed.
Hearts inflamed
The spirit untamed,
Exuberant and unashamed.

This love
Is not for the shadow above-
The hordes caprice-
But for the silent peace
Where the soul finds eternal rest
And there is no need to be blest
No need for an inquest
Sin and shame and disdain
They had their chance-
Guilt with every glance,
Eschewed at last
For that heavenly embrace
Of passion unchaste.

Foresworn to God
They missed their chance
For a sensual embrace,
Free of sin
And the need to repent.

If they could awaken
From the sleep of death
And see they were forsaken
By the ministers' deliberations.
Appalled by their decay
In their silent dismay

and disappointment -
Left behind for cold viewing
by their earthly guests.

The hallowed forgotten-
An insurgent plea of discontentment
Would rise over their dissolution
And wayward compensation.

Their resting bones
Would be their home
Their spirits without resolution,
Their deeds proffering no absolution,
Their prayers and salutations
Left in graves along with their illusions.

Death Is Never Remiss

Death is never remiss.
It can never be dismissed.
It's never absent
Late or early.
It's always on time and orderly -
One hundred percent reliable.
Even Hume could not misconstrue
That it's a priori true.
It's never unpredictable
Or held accountable -
When the bell rings.
There is no reckoning
Or misgiving
With this infallible ending.
It cares not who is next in line -
It's a definitive design.
It has no need for remorse for its deeds,
Or strive for ambition or Self-esteem,
Or deem it necessary to be forgiven,
Or seek adulation for being dependable
Punctual or infallible.
No need for self-esteem
In its iron-clad scheme.
No medals are needed for a painless demise
Or blame for an insufferable end -
Its all the same -
There is no one to blame;
It's clearly an inscrutable plan.

Birth

Waiting for the cry of death
Paroxysm of pain to cease
And the shocking breath of life released-
The squalling bairn comes forth at last
The cord of life is severed fast,
blood spurts, with a throbbing heart,
a sturdy clamp staves off death -
and its fearful stealth.
Alas! a terror-stricken gaze loses its sway
and the aftermath of pus and amniotic fluid is wiped away,
after the contractions eased their fray.
A sanctuary of the flesh –
the infant is pressed against his mother's breast - easing its distress.
Held so lovingly - his mother's smile so bold,
But lo and behold his fate is foretold,
his first breath portends his death
each is counted one by one
until the casket claims her son.
After many a sunrise the earth did greet
The furnace put him in a dusty retreat
in an urn until his remains the wind did meet
his life was gladly lent but quickly spent.

An Explosive Affair

Propane loves a little tickle
One that isn't fickle
And waltzes with air
In tight quarters
Until there is a flare.
It can be a quick affair -
A shuffling of fumes and a little O2,
Makes a perfect brew
Or a worthy coup -
partners with a rendezvous.
Love at first sight - then it blew.
Everyone in its wake flew
Like a bouncer tossing an irate drunk in a funk
by the seat of his pants
Headlong without a glance.
These lovers want their solitude -
No one to menace them when they collude -
A consummation of an unpredictable magnitude.
Meddlers are unwelcome –
Those that loiter waiting for the bedlam.
Those unthinking fools
That miss the clues.
Not a whit of manners,
No cordial goodbyes,
Or friendly winks-
Just up and out they went -
Through windows or doors.
Known for a mean demeanor when stoked,
Impolite when provoked.
Won't revoke
Any heartless deed
Won't repent when its victims are bruised or dead.
No amends for their sins
Atonement for blasting a fleeing victim into a wall
When rushing down a hall -
temper tantrums are expected –
Avoid them when you can;
They can vary -
Unleash a red-hot fury
Or a mere unsavory "poof".

Before these lovers unite
One can be impolite,
Exudes a stench before orgiastic delight -
A hint to escape – don't take a chance
And hang around for a dance.
Run at last before the first blast -
Beware! before it burns you to a crisp.
Least of all, don't be rude and ignore the call.
They are bullies when the two unite -
Pack a deadly punch - don't skip the hunch
Or risk being expunged.
Keep these lovers apart
They call the shots – keep them confined
Don't satisfy their needs - Armageddon might be at hand.
They are sneaky – one creeps under foot without a care
Hovers about with a silent dare
Waiting patiently for a lover's caress –
Any flirtatious spark that wanders by.
Once these lovers come together
Curbing the wrath or fitful anger
Is a fruitless endeavor -
Best to avoid the entanglement altogether;
This affair could be disaster.
A lucky few have tempered the lovers' effusion -
A fire extinguisher spared them from a quick journey to the hereafter.
A little affection rather than a prolonged affair
Won't bring much of a fanfare.
A prolonged affair
Can bring a clarion call
And a legion of men to quell
One of its capricious spells.
If ethane tips the scales,
Don't be surprised if you sail.
If good fortune prevails
And that nuisance stench lingers still
Don't flip a switch or strike a match -
You'll see eternity after a breathless dispatch.

Evil Is Ordained

I Came With Auschwitz

Bombing raids could not be heard
Nor the screams from those gas chambers of death -
Evil spoke without redress -
As I lingered in the womb of sleep
Before my lungs took flight with breath
I dreamed in darkness in this restful retreat.
Spared the sinister rumors of nihilism and deceit -
Of those twisted tales of genocide,
And those iniquitous showers of cyanide,
For those instant graves of gypsies and Jews
Neither God nor man could undue.
I heard nothing
Of love and hate
Or the winged bullets
Perforating flesh
Unclenched fists
Of dying men
In swirling blood, in agony and torment,
Crying out in heaven's breach -
Who dares beseech?
God's tarnished song
Dares not any liaison
Between heaven and earth.
The risen chalice - the purity of the host
Was lost in the dust
That blew over those unmarked graves of the holocaust.
I came with Auschwitz
Swept from the womb of silence
And took my first breath
As those took there's with Zyklon B.
I will keen interminably
For the lost lineage
Without name or stone
Only their withered bones
Of those bulldozed into trenches.
The horror of the past
Touches our soul askance -
Never enough to foster a perennial stance.

Evil

Flowers grow above their graves
Nothing left at Auschwitz to engrave.
Old tattered bones trellised together in Nazi tombs -
Sort them out and claim them as your own -
This montage of bones only God could sort and bemoan
The evil that was done
Under the sun
That will never shine again -
With so much disdain and so much pain.
Extermination was the theme
Crematoriums filled with Zyklon B
Used to bath them in a hazy dream of death
Until they had no breath.
They raked cement walls-
Fingernails ripped off as they clawed –
Stubs bleeding in desperate clinching,
Left in breathless flinching
Lungs seared with cyanide gas.
Canisters of death killed en masse -
Millions In those exterminating "muffles"-
Disposable victims of Nazi shovels
After the industrial slaughter
Deloused the dead.

Their eyes bulged as they took their last gasp.
Their hair was clipped
Their gold teeth were stolen
To leverage a sullen reward
When the Wannsee accord was proffered
With a goodwill toast and hearty applaud
The Final Solution was deemed unflawed.
These soulless images of stacked and nameless bodies
Sprinkled with lye to decompose them fast
As bulldozers hide their heartless deeds in dark graves, at last.
Below the grass and flowers as we count the hours
Bones lost in the sunbaked dirt
Their dreams deferred
Names still drift across ancient lips
Without a face to see or a hand to hold.
A story that must be told
Of a dispirited degradation

Of limitless despair without libation.
The dead and their dusty remains
Will torture the conscience of the living with shame
And haunt the dreams of savage beasts.
A flower in the field will redeem
Those unmarked graveyard pits of lost dreams
Where hairless corpses in heaps reside -
Their stories denied.

The Towers

Steel melted like lava from a volcano,
Concrete turned to dust and ashes - a jet fueled inferno.
Two smoldering towers collapsed into powder,
Gnarled spokes of rebar - dark and brittle,
Like a phalanx of dead twisted vines poked up in the haze of confusion and soot.
Some chose to be incinerated,
Scorched in the safe confines of melting steel and crumbling mortar,
Enveloped in a blanket of smoke and flames,
And swoon in the tumbling blaze.
The window leapers avoided cremation and took flight:
Twisting raveling and hurling through space - rag dolls with flailing arms –
Rather be crushed on cement than burn with those blaring alarms.
A terror ridden plunge,
A merciful asphyxiation,
Before the imminent collision - better than cremation -
A sudden skull-busting mist of sanguine or ruby red -
A rainbow in sunlight.
One after the other falling like wounded birds -
A steady rhythm of misty prism and crushed bones.
What was left it the debris and dust? –
The powered remains of aluminum, steel, mortar, and bones mixed with jet fuel,
Lost souls stir and poke through the corrupt cesspool,
Hoping to find a skull or a trinket that might be a clue -
Anything for a loved one to make a decree
From that volcanic debris.
They bartered their lives for a dusty settlement,
Masterminded their self-serving jet-fueled holocaust,
Created rainbows out of blood,
Turned flesh and bone into dust,
Left cynical smiles for the world to admire or despise.

The Spindle – a True Story

There he lay – dead,
Blood oozing from his head
A desk spike impaled in his eye,
The morning custodian did descry -
A gruesome sight without contrite.
Thrust so deep the spindle went
Puncturing the brain with disdain and pitiless intent -
It was plain to see it was a ruthless incident.
The detectives had never seen such a savage event -
"How unpleasant. Must've died in an instant", came the first comment.
"What a ruthless way for a life to be spent - what torment!"
Another said with sober lament.
The weapon used had a guileless intent - a spindle spike
And a single thrust is all it took –
An unrivaled feat that ended a life with a single stroke.
A scene both wanton and unique – meant to provoke
There he lay across his desk –
So Kafkaesque
Sprawled out across his desk -
A spindle spike lodged in his eye -
A spectacle to terrible to rectify.
Mouth ajar, his face contorted in a bewildering shock -
Nothing to mock - a dead psychiatrist in his white frock.
His arms outstretched like a man on a cross,
Bloody receipts covering his face,
Held in tact by the spindle's base,
Belied the pathos and the sadistic twist to the case -
But no matter the humorous hints or irony on display,
Or the cynical and convoluted turns that might dismay,
Thy questions remained- who was to blame?
Who had the gull and where withal?
To drive an antique paper spike into a psychiatrist's eye?
Who Left the kindly old Freudian Analyst to die? -
Who, like a priest, listened to a litany of suffering that never ceased;
Who sat for hours ensconced in his oak chair without much flair,
And listened to Mary speak of her despair over her affair,
Heeded those with obsessive thoughts that held them in a snare
Tended to those who heard voices that impaired their welfare.
Heard their tales of woe and cured their afflictions
With the right prescriptions.
Even though he did his best, did one of his patients become a pest?

Enraged enough to grasp the base and ram a spindle into his face?
Did lithium fail to temper the mania and cause a fight?
Did valium fail to curb a rage filled flight?
Did a schizophrenic panic -
Thought his drugs were spiked with arsenic?
Could any one of these beleaguered souls commit such a dastardly deed?
Were they incapable of such a plot?
The detectives wondered – mired in thought.
Not so, the detectives knew they were incapable of such a plot.
Those absconded drugs were no afterthought.
Several addicts took the prize,
They rightfully surmised – an after-hour surprise -
Of hucksters, hustlers of ill-repute wanting easy highs -
Caught him at his desk reviewing his patients' notes.
He rose with a startled stare before a word was spoke
The agile of the two - distraught at getting caught –
Grabbed the spindle off the desk and plunged it in his eye.
Such a menacing attack was easy to track:
It was certain no patient committed such an act –
A salient clue provided a breakthrough -
The shelves were empty and ransacked for valium and Prozac;
This wasn't a petulant patient looking for payback -
Or one to hoard so many drugs to sell in a single bushwhack.
No - it was an unprincipled knave with this kind of knack -
To leave a man to die
With a four-inch spindle in his eye.

What evil crushes a man's will
With urges he seems so willing to fulfill
And sends him on a wreck less path without restraint
And tests the noble mettle of man or saint?
Is it temptation or fate that makes him take the bait?
Something set in stone already condoned by fate
Or ordained by God without debate -
Neither will or desire can dispel?
Something in his nature that casts a spell? -
A bane that can't be explained
That makes him corruptible and vain.
Once unleashed his evil deeds never wane -
Neither God or man can explain.

Mountain Climbers

Nature sets the scales – obey or die
Governs life and death - useless to decry.
A sudden overcast can steal a sunny day.
Even worse - flood a lowly mountain town.
Pompeii was wiped out in a day
After Mt. Vesuvius had its say.
Nature's wrath with sudden dismay
Can spawn instant melee.
Bury the unsuspecting in a mountain of snow or clay.
Three climbers perished on Mt hood one wintry day -
Lost their way –
Hiking up toward a heavenly sky
When the sun bore no light to lead the way.
A blizzard created quite a fray
Waylaid their joyful task
Left them blind with a frozen mask.
Scattered like snowflakes in the wind
Floundering in the frozen tundra unaligned
One found refuge in a snow glistened tomb,
A primitive igloo forged by hand to avoid impending doom.
Desperately swinging his pick to forestall a certain death -
His frost-bitten fingers piled sparkling flakes into an arching wall,
A frozen cave to retire –
Hoping in his frantic dredging not to expire.
Immured in a cold silence –
Willfully defiant -
In his womb of frozen crystals
Awaiting his death in his crystalline castle.
His companions of ice and snow
Mingled about in frantic gusto.
Two perished in an icy meadow –
Buried in a silent crypt of ice and snow -
A soft sepulcher of frozen blood -
Covered with a blanket of slush.
Preserved in a likely embrace,
Frozen like the lovers on the Grecian Urn -
Mummified by snow and ice - never to return.
One escaped - begging nature not to forsake
Clamoring not to be a frozen keepsake.
Spared a wind-swept death
And faced the horror of nature's savage hand –

But the wind and ice portends.
A feeble snow pack took three and made no amends -
The lonely mountain's constant friends
Companions in ice and snow.
One rests in his homemade tomb,
The other two were locked in an icy cave –
Tightly stuffed in the blizzard's unmarked grave.
Nothing fancy but preserves the dead -
Will do as gravesites go
No burial ground where tears can flow
No loved ones to bid farewell.
No weeping rituals to send them heaven bound –
Mere incarnations in a frozen ground,
Preserved interminably from sun or sky –
Loved ones' memories they can't defy -
A shadow cast upon time they can't belie.
The date is marked when it went awry.

Perchance curious hikers will stumble onto their icy graves
A millennium might pass and they'll be found at last –
An archeologist's dream -
Mystified by what they find
Lovers embraced in sleepy repose,
One resting alone
Beguiled by a mountain storm.

Prisoner of Shadows

We are prisoners of shadows
We hide in the crepuscular light
Of moonless nights.
Dark shadows serve us best.
As we pursue our timeless craft
Sunlight must never shine on our path
For we will be greeted with scorn and wrath.
We must remain forever in the shade
To sweat and toil with our weary trade
Our efforts merit no praise
No stars will bear our name
We are smitten by our claim
Even when we drive no fame
As our labor continues in vain.
We are not to be shamed
If our craft is ordained and unrestrained.
And portends dire ends.

Wistful urges stir in our veins
And we grasp those poetic strains
That foment from our tormented brains
And manifest from the shadows to reign
Our brow is hot with sweat
But our labor only brings regret,
And more deploring threats
From those plebian wits
Declaring us rebels gone amiss!
With their ignoble deeds
And heartless creeds
they thwart our bliss
As we labor in the abyss -
Of those shadows that shield us from hypocrites.
We are tormented by dejection
Hope our words could be accepted
In a world corrupt and deceptive
Filled with the zealot's blame
And the fanatic's aim -
Those assassin's disdain.
We are like peasants in a field
Bent over, our faces never seen
Fearing too much sunlight might disclose our fears

And the mockery and sneers
At our fruitless labor – perennially out of favor.
Should we set a date and spurn our fate? --
Our eristic voice is strong
But no one listens to our song -
Even when our verses make a dent,
And our souls are spent,
There is nothing to show for our assent -
Only a perennial discontent.
Neither a farthing or a cent,
Adulation or lament
Is proffered for our consent
And leave us content.
We wanted to warn -
Not be scorned or spurned -
And heed our word,
And let us spar
From the shadows
With those creeds
That spur those false decrees.

Those who dared to peer in the shadows
To expose and glare at our metaphors -
Handiwork of the soul -
Saw the shifting paradigms difficult to troll,
Saw the old ones still chocking in the dust,
Saw the new ones looked upon with disgust -
Each sucked the marrow from ancient bones
To renew a barren land
Where nothing grows, but what is merely bland.
Weeds can flourish on this loom;
The poets' seeds when blown upon the ground -
fertile and sound -
Struggle when sown
And cannot bloom
In soil that remains infertile and doomed.
We keep planting among the weeds.
What else can we do with our seeds? -
With those that were planted by our hand
After a great deal of toil on this barren land,
As they lie quietly, reposing in the soil
Like little tombs that are doomed,
We wish could bloom.

The sun can't warm them,
Water can't reach root or stem -
They die - no laurels or a diadem.
No sorrow is spared;
No one even cared
To have the seed spared
To see the flower flared,
No loss or death despaired
Or misspent labor declared.
In the shadows - our chosen lot -
we retain our dignity – forever sought-
Planting seeds sipping brandy and coffee -
Hoping one will bloom – our modus operandi.

We continue to plant in barren soil;
To nourish a flower after our toil
On this stark and desolate land
Where only the lowly cacti can stand.
Little is known of our suffering,
And why we stay in the shadows dreaming -
Prisoners of an ineffable yearning
To plant our seeds in the meadows
To cultivate flowers
In a barren land.

Canto II

Inspired by the past
Our verses crafted from hand me downs -
Old flowers we pondered in the desolate land.
In the shadows like the rest - we tried our hand
To wrench from this barren land
A flower of our own like those that still stand -
A little taller or a little shorter, perhaps,
But nonetheless a worthy digress.
Sheer off this
Pluck that
We did our best
To make our mark with our seeds in the desert sand
And grow a flower in this barren land
As our predecessors had.
Whether we hide in shadows or take a stand
Face down our assassins as they kick and brand -

We won't wilt in this waste land.
Dreams tug at our soul -
Oneiric fragments -
Verses, hallowed and intransient.
When We are excoriated with disdain,
Denied any praise,
Deprived of fame -
The stars don't bear our name -
We continue to labor in vain.
Those wistful urges still stir in our veins
We still toil from the shadows to reign.
When the brow is hot with sweat
Our labor only brings more threats,
From those paragoned wits
Who chastises us as amiss -
Their ignoble deeds and pretentious decrees
Thwart our bliss.
Sometimes a sanguine voice can be heard
Over the desert storms of hot sun and sand
Urging us to plant in this scorched land
Those inchoate seeds that have been banned.
The land is so barren little can blend,
When whispers of mediocrity are in the wind;
We must follow the voice when our muse is inclined;
And preserver as those seeds are refined,
And trust we aren't maligned.
We trim and add to a weary paradigm -
And cast our seed in the barren land
And let it ripen among the vines and groves of man -
And leaves the weak and blind behind
And their shallow urges for the divine
And their dogmatic chime of the penitent's bell -
A cruel spell
That wages shame,
enthralls the weak with blame.
I will come out of the shadow,
Read my cursed verses
And let time be my judge and executioner.
Then let me be laid to rest
After years of showing my unrest
To what I could attest
Let the ages declare
What I refused to spare.

Canto III

Can we ever emerge from the shadows?
celebrate an invocation
walk into the light and proclaim a revelation-
face our mortality
And rid ourselves of the dirge of incense
Lamentations pleading for recompense.
Death is a long slumber we can't amend,
Pontificate about or ascend.
Out of the darkness we can transcend
Implore our nature and not offend.
Let Reason and the poet's wager blend
Religion has nothing to portend
just useless rituals that make us pretend
That salvation, a prolific coy, can our sins resend.
The shallow-minded and the weak-willed still rule-
Biased fools!
Blind to reason and the lips of old
The minions fold
Until the unctuous creeds are told
stuck in a groove
A broken record grinding out the same old tune-.

God invites his flock to heaven and warns them against hell before they reach the tomb-
Where, prophets contend, good souls and sinners go when life comes to an end;
For those who are a blend
Purgatory is a choice many commend.
But candles must be lit on their behalf,
Otherwise, limbo is their cast.
Commiserating is better than falsehood
Love and loss is ever present
And fear of death is unpleasant-
Our beliefs in God and heaven never ease these penchants.
Death is never celebrated in joy and relief
Over the soul's release-
Let's have a beer and celebrate my wife's death without the slightest regret.
Reason and science is as close to heaven as we will ever get
They've done more to ease our pain and provide comfort than religion ever has-
Certainly done more good than God's original plan.
After all, it was man who cured the sick and feed the flock.

He, instead, left us to our own demise
Where we had to devise-
Lacking in advice-
Our crafty ways to counter his cruel vice.
If God aided us in our scheme to thrive
He left myriads to suffer before he disclosed to us our enlightenment.

Magical Kingdom

Few enter the Magical Kingdom
It's not a place for divine wisdom
Inspiration or hope.
It's the word salad bunch
Lost in their listless hallucinations and thoughts
Where the world is a delusional hoax.
Ruled by white coats
With jingling keys
That open thick doors to the enchanted kingdom -
Hades delight –
God's blight
On a misguided dominion
Where the rulers of the kingdom
Dispense ecstasy –
Zestfully -
In those colored pills of clemency
To those lost souls waiting in line for their angry fix
To unscramble neurons that play psychic tricks -
See how God gets His kicks -
On helpless victims transfixed -
In His cruel and preordained eclipse.
Voices are heard without a person speaking a word.
Despondency undeterred -suicidal impulses spurred.
Futile acts - ceaseless and robotic –
Sorely chaotic -
repetitious as a broken record.
Hallucinations that appear like ghosts
That haunt the spirit when they are evoked.
Manic highs that toss the psyche into a fit
Gamble away money in a single sit
Fly to New York and see Lindbergh takeoff -
Sure no one would scoff.

To cease those reckless neurons
Those pills are often not enough
The white-coated rulers have more up their sleeve
Another secret that might relieve
Those misdirected synapses that skip and bereave.
Trundle those selected few on gurney wheels -
Stoned on propofol or methohexital pills-
Down the narrow hall

Settled good and tall
Mouth piece in between the jaws
Ready to ascend one of God's ungrateful faux pas.
A simple press of a button scrambles the brain -
A reprieve from the worldly strain –
An electrocution that has no shame
When reason suspends
Those delusions and schizophrenic trends
And those neurons are whipped back in shape!
Their tongues are held in place with wooden sticks,
As rulers heave on their chests
until they breathe again -
resurrected from the dead -
So, let them splurge with an ECT surge
They buck like broncos when flesh and current converge
Dreams and memories are erased after the purge -
The soul is at peace after the pulse ridden upsurge
Those neurons rebel and the demons return
To cast their diabolical spell.
Pills are dispersed to fight against God's neurological doom.
Lithium, and Thorazine are just a few that suppress the gloom -
Trick the neurons from slipping out of place
A bipolar or mania disgrace
Voices when there is no one to embrace
Ceaseless depression that can't be displaced.

When ECT and pills fail to quell
their moody spells -
They are stuffed in padded cells.
Like a monk's retreat, a mat for sleep
a shaft of sunlight as a friend.
A reprieve, they contend, to curb the wanton demons that offend.
Their transgressions are not their own -
they do not have to atone
But imprisonment they are prone
Until another round of ETC
Or a higher dosage spree.
There are no means to convalesce and heal –
Those baleful afflictions can never be beset
With any means that can offset
Those neurons that are preset.

What is gained by these malicious diseases?
Does God have His malicious reasons?
to cancel a worthy remedy for this mental treason? -
cruelty without reason.
A chemical respite curtails the agony -
A temporary reprieve from this psychological savagery.
ECT quells the synaptic debauchery -
A false hope that soon lapses.
No remedy is at hand to mitigate their wretched plight.
Putting a clamp on dopamine may curb the psychotic twilight.
Haldol may curb those unwanted voices –
But strokes and panic attacks are a likely counterpoise.
The same is true for mania and depression
Until blurred vision, convulsions and impotence make an impression.
Paranoia is gone with Thorazine
but it slows the heart and fainting begins.
Lithium too can subdue mercurial displays and mania
a natural element by nature's hand -
it's too toxic and not very grand -
more maladies manifest to undermine the quest:
seizures and comas possess the unblessed;
but there's more to implicate the drug:
Trembling hands are a common complaint
Until a cardiac arrest tosses in the final restraint.
No matter their fate - ECT or drugs, padded cell or restraints-
The afflicted can't escape their mental constraints,
duped by God, man drifts in an unwieldly current
a prey to nature's misguided torrent -
God and man fail to find a deterrent -
No divine or earthly circuit -
Silent cruelty from above,
Muddled confusion from below.
Those minions clad in white
those clinicians with a higher stripe
classify their cripples
with accurate and astute labels
Yet lack a worthy solution.
Who's to blame for such shame?
Without an aim Man isn't to blame.
His tools are lame;
His means are too tame
To fight God's evil game.
The plague did destroy before we found a ploy

Polio did cripple and kill until IPV was employed -
Both put an end to a baleful fate.
Diphtheria had its way
until DPT put an end to its cruel domain.
We found a way to curb God's willful depravity,
Yet those diseases of the soul remain unspent – a steadfast enmity.
No remedies at hand conquer the mental twists
that prey upon the mind.
God, at last, has run us aground
With a barbaric antipathy that resolutely resounds.

Paradise Lost

Darwin doused the flames of Christendom
Reduced it to embers
That some still want to rekindle
Even make them comingle
Only one flame will linger -
Accused of being sinful
For showing favor
For beasts of prey
Rather than a savior
From an unconsummated birth
Sent to earth to save the curst,
Proclaim creeds of damnation and sin to unnerve,
Extol myths and dreams to preserve
Exalt a soul to rescue so it can serve
A redeemer and a divine plan
And become God's fan.
Claim the earth no older than a clam
Science is the devil's scam -
Milton's screed to save God's plan.

Variation is the rightful game
Inheritance and selection make their claim
Selection is the ultimate aim
Not sin, degradation and shame.
There's no unconsummated dame
Or a rock pushing cave-man,
Who opened heaven's gate
We have to emulate -
To be saved as sinful ingrates.
There was no paradise
To lose or gain
As Milton proclaimed.
Life was not preordained
That was magically fixed
Uncarved by time -
Each thing already designed -.
An anagalid to a rat
A miacis to a bear
None were here ready -made
Set in time
By God's hand.

From the ocean we came
Slime and muck
Genes to be plucked
And survival to be plucked –
A matter of luck.
Fins becomes legs
Teeth become beaks
Feathers become wings -
All to survive
And keep the species alive.

Divine providence holds no sway,
No need to beg or pray
To be redeemed to keep the devil away.
Dispel any thoughts of original sin
to punish a sinful lot without end.
No benevolent chaperon watches over Camelot
Or an ill-tempered judge of our evil plot,
No angels about to render support
After God has taken his punishing shots -
Draw a line between the dots
Selection saves the lot
Divination is a false plot -
personification and myth contrive
to hypnotize the tribe
To believe a tale of ignoble pride
Where lusting after sin and degradation is fortified.

Good and evil exists is in the heart of man
One or the other can have the upper hand –
Both struggle for the rightful domain -
Nevertheless, by their own command.
No God above to add a reprimand.
It's a back-yard brawl -
Evolution determines the draw.
Winner takes all.
Nature shuffles the cards –
It's not a game of chance
Without a prerequisite glance
It's determined by who can make the dance
When genes are shuffled in advance.
The strong hold the crown and fair out the best

The weak are not blessed
Eliminated when they fail the primary test.
The world is a barbaric feast
Conquer or be conquered – a meal for the beast -
Not for the priest.
Slave or master until one is deceased.
Salvaged for slaughter and a barbaric feast.
The Jackal eats the remains the pride left behind
A crippled antelope is eaten alive
It couldn't thrive.
A butterfly is picked off by a hungry bird
Later devoured by a hawk – survival of the fittest confirmed.
An endless feast of death – nature's way preferred.
When the quota is filled, the hungry fed,
The cycle postponed until the grumbling is heard.
Morsels of the dead
Consumed in horror and dread
Until the strong are fed.
The fittest see the morning sun
It's an unfolding dance,
The weak perish, the effete are given another chance
Combinations that can be shaken
If the species needs to awaken -
A natural equation of what can be conquered
Mutating to see what can be outnumbered.
Genetic shuffling determines our fate -
Who will be picked off and who will incarnate?
The pilgrimage stays afloat for those who acclimate -
Who wins the contest for the strongest mate -
And wasn't conned of the best genetic wand
And wasn't eaten at dawn after being spawned -
A beast of prey, rarely preyed upon.
The Kingdom where the weak are pawned -
Too chilling a place for providence to lay claim
Or a God to praise or blame.
To live or not to live is the eschatological scheme
Success of the kill - take out the feeble or the lame -
The impotent are put to shame,
Not the helpless sinners who need to be framed.
This is a charade – they too are cast in the same barbaric shade -
To be conquered or conquer is the name of the game.
The long-tongued frog reeling in a bug
The cobra's paralyzing bite is no bluff -

Take a life in an instant strike - that's chilling enough
Better yet - hyenas feasting on a corpse,
Ripping and tearing the blood-soaked fur – depicting its brutal force
A tireless struggle for the last remaining morsel
Their jaws are wide and their mouths engorged
The fiendish look in their eyes show no remorse.
It's a world sparse of love and charity
Void of redemption from sin or God's purity.
We are no better off than the weasel or the rat
We are creatures of nature's whim
We are just as grim
When we kill and maim.
Ready with weapons to kill lurking prey –
Be it man or beast we wish to assay
To kill or carry away.
We scheme as well
With might to kill -
Whether to eat or retaliate.
It's a heartless campaign
For beast or man
All needing to feast on demand.
The machinations of nature always prevail.
To see who will live or fail.
Sin and redemption - a useless tale -
Clergyman devise - a senseless travail.

VISIONS AND HALLUCINATIONS

Candlelight

A candle's wavering flame delights,
the best companion on lonely nights,
illuminating a dark and lonely room
rescues a man marooned
awash in an obsidian tide of darkness.
Its flickering luminosity
portends a romantic prophesy
for a sensuous interlude
that transcends the lascivious or the lewd.
The skin may sweat
the exuberant moans spent
passions and promises unbent
hallowed in the flickering light -
ever so bright.

Betrayal comes with an unexpected breeze –
its fateful nemesis -
stifles it in its concluding exodus.
A burned-out wick
Betrays its consent
it had to relent –
worn from age and overuse -
it expires from hours of thoughtless abuse –
suffocating in melting wax -
a cruel and heartless climax,
when the flame expires
snuffed into oblivion
after its desperate delirium.

Loyal to its last quivering flutter,
it heaved its last breath with a quick and final stutter,
departing those entwined lovers -
their rubicund bodies left in the shadows
their sweltering passion squandered in the darkness
those primitive dreams left in their slumbering souls.

Candles burn in nightly rooms
as the moon
drifts across the sky on its sullen path -
not to be surpassed -.
as it waits in suspense

for its chance
to see those candles rest
after their test
from their flickering delirium -
before they slip into oblivion -
So, it can cast its crepuscular gaze
Upon those lovers spent in the shadowy maze.

The Mask

A nightly candle flickered bold and bare.
Its yellow flame burned space and air;
Invaded the shadows with an imposing dare.
Dreams and visions seemed to heat my brain with every flare.
Revelations appeared in the eye of the flame
Mesmerized I faced a threshold I was coerced to endure,
Teeming with ecstasy alluring and obscure,
The eye of the flame held steady and pure
I was sent me reeling into another world –
A mirror of my soul that I thought put me in peril.
The candle flickered once again –
a dance between air and flame
So beguiling I couldn't refrain.
A solitary night of visions stirred me so
I wondered what they could bestow -
As crystalline colors sent me swirling with vertigo.
The candle flickered again and I was resigned
To a remain gazing into the flame's cosmic eye.
In one hallowed flick I could descry
A shadow and light interplay in a hypnotic display
That seized my brain.
The candle flickered rapidly -
Choking in melting wax -
Like a drowning man gasping for air -
It continued to flicker and fad as if caught in snare.
A haze of smoke emerged in the darkness – floating nebulous and serene
A face appeared and drifted in the misty cloud like a floating figurine.
A death mask, white as chalk with blood shot eyes, leered at me,
disembodied - bobbing like a balloon on string.
Our eyes locked and I fell into a trance -
Fixed and unable to shed its eerie glance.
It spoke as if from afar like a voice emanating from a dark crevasse.
its lips moved slowly and I was hypnotized by its chant.
As it spoke, I seemed stranded in a sempiternal impasse.
"Fear me not. I am you in the shadow of destiny. You have fractured time and are in a wayward and eternal moment. You've discovered the other side of yourself in the Cosmic Eye, you are in your soul – the mirror of your inner self; I can't betray you, for I am you."
His voice was like an echo from long ago.
Held in abeyance until it could bestow
A hidden secret it had to sow.

But was it real - a thing to behold that would unfold?
Or was it a mere vision in his brain that was foretold? -
He'd never know the strength of its hold.
Whether it was seed of his own
A hallucination of my brain alone
Or brought to me in a dream –
Endemic of another world -
A seed of its own –
I can't determine which I should behold.
The entity from his dream spoke again
With the same distant voice
Compelled to listen - mesmerized by its cunning ploy
It weaved back and forth in a frightful haste
Daring me to be unbraced -
"Transcend this place!"
"Merge with the cosmic eye – fear not its embrace" -
"Fear not its decree –
It will set you free!"
It was like the face of death effulgent in its ghastly luminosity
And sported a spirited smile with a spiteful jocosity.
Its piercing blood shot eyes bulged
As it persisted its erratic dancing about the obsidian room.
Then it ceased in midair
Fixed itself for one final stare
Intending to mortify
And vanished in the cosmic eye
Like a shooting star in a night sky
The melting wax smothered the flame
Flickering faster and faster like dying man
Gasping for air as death clutches his hand
A silence prevailed it had no more demands -
The spiritual dictum was over.
It had no more to offer.
Frazzled by the frenzy of the vision
He drifted into a dreamless sleep.
He awoke with a sudden start after a transfigured night.
He wondered if the candle light held the secret to his life
And the cosmic eye would appear again in the heart of the flame.

Eye of the Kundalini

A sacred force that slumbers low,
Erupts like a volcano,
Rushes up the spine -
A perfect flume for the eternal flame.
A dormant energy until it shows
How it awakens no one knows
Often spontaneous it begins to glow
Shaking loose an ancient power,
Striking each chakra on the tower -
The great reservoir of primordial fire,
Lifts the spirit - dampens desire.
When it hits the final wheel,
A golden sunset appears and a great star is unsealed
A pyric maze of bliss revealed.
Amber rivers flow with a luminous grace,
And dreams of ancient kingdoms haunt my nightly rest,
Rendering a munificent pageantry of life and death -
Caves bearing skulls of brethrens past,
Forlorn and forsaken in the dust;
Their cryptic drawings on damp walls extols their spirit,
Transcends this cruel and hapless life.

It's a furious flame delivered high
From a burning cauldron below -
A flash of the white light, a spark of life
The pulse up the spine
That hallowed fulmination in the brain
That can't be explained.
Transposed just the same,
I heard voices from long ago
I could not forego
That spoke of a heavenly vision so sublime -
That it transcended time -
Cast in hues of blue and azure in its prime
It had no paradigm.
My soul was on fire;
Reason circumscribed;
The transcendent inscribed;
An imprint forged;
A mystical odyssey prevailed
To the Golden Temple – my soul unveiled
In the eternal eye of the Kundalini.

Peyote Vision

Popped a button or two
Saw a heavenly view,
An angel of destiny that couldn't be subdued
A white serpent warped around her neck tightly bound
Draped over her bosoms – an image breathless and spellbound.
The brain did burst with an ebullient spark
Bearing the flame of ecstasy, I did depart,
In a weightless buoyancy of heart.
I seemed to float in a cosmic space
As seraphic images did happen by,
Quicker than the blink of an eye -
Fiery image of yellow and red with a golden glow,
Sparkling bright like a halo
Inside were unfurled white wings ready for flight
Nearly blinding my sight.
Icarus floated by –
His auric winged arms outstretched -
Soaring heavenward.
Suddenly a voice spoke - clear and loud -
"Open this cosmic diary!" it said, stentorian and bold,
Penetrating through a misty cloud.
"Memorize these numbers!", it stressed –
An imploring tone that startled my soul I had to confess.
So, I did as I was told,
And sealed them in place
That I could trace.
Once embraced
They disappeared into an indigo sky.
A tumbler as on a safe floated by
With shinny numbers glowing translucent -
Flashing and glimmering for my amusement,
Until lightening rumbled through the indigo sky
And a voice declared "Turn the dial!"
I shuttered so and spun it with curious intent -
It seemed those numbers bore a hopeful portent -
I chuckled when I thought
The universe could be unlocked –
"It's true!" the voice remarked.
So, I twisted the tumbler – a safe cracker's delight -
And felt the naked yearning of a solemn plight,
And felt the cosmos unite with a refulgent light.

A golden hue that shimmered with such delight.
I knew, at once, time took flight –
It was so sublime
That the muted clicking urged me to seek the divine.
I opened the door and heard a transcendent refrain,
That voice intervened again with a rhythm ordained
"I am the wave the universe serves"
"The eternal presence where everything returns"
"I wrote the script for a cosmic journal."
"All things are in it – every luminescent moment" -
"An infant's cry",
"A mother's lullaby",
"A dying man's sullen goodbye",
"The hunger in a wolf's eye", -
"A celestial script that will mystify."
I turned each page as if to pry
With a Goldeneye
Until time was unspent
And there was no one to console or lament.
I found a marked page –
Bent in the corner that seemed to have no age.
It was the manuscript to my soul
Suddenly I lost control
And became the voice I heard;
Nothing stirred but the silent word
As I was consumed by the Golden Flame
I could not tame
As mescaline took over my brain.

The Kundalini

Serpent of fire, the seed of the Golden Light
In a flame that bolted up my spine and did ignite
An illumination in my brain so bright
I was transfixed by its splendor I took flight
Into that Golden Light
With amber halos all around mixed in an azure cloud.
The torrent was strong and nothing had gone wrong
The unimpeded force hit the brain headstrong.
I lay in a captivated bliss I couldn't resist -
This sudden vision in the night gave me such a fright.
I seemed to float - an unknown presence - in the stream of time –
I could see as if an eclipsed declined
Dusty hearths in caves of long ago
Skeletons and skulls - remains of brethren of a lost domain.
Time disposed of them
Left them there -
Their lives over quicker than a flickering flame
Where time and the elements were to blame.
Rituals staked their claim
Their drawings on cavern walls no one could defame –
Left from the serpent's flame.
They saw the purple light and the golden haze
In spectral objects and halo glances as I had seen.
In silent moments, they heard a voice from within the darkened den,

Felt its presence dwelling deep within the cavern's core
It spoke to them of a secret lore
like Perseus from a far off shore.
They ate and drank from their dead kens' skulls,
Hoping the spirits from the dead would call
And the serpent over-ride the eclipse of death
And the muse be sustained on cavern walls
Those fiery drawings did enthrall.
As the sacred man did draw,
They sat around an earthen fire of repose
An eternal watch they thought was exposed.
As I dreamed in my restless repose
From their portal home I could see,
A door way to a mountain dome,
And azure skies and horizons clear as glass
With shafts of sunbursts when clouds dispersed, at last.

I peered, as they, at misty rains where little rills did drain,
And crepuscular flowers that in their wind-blown shimmering did astound
Saw frozen winter grounds where icy lakes abound,
And hot copper skies where nothing can be disguised -
And mirages rise high.
We saw with awe the crepuscular light of dawn,
Where the interplay of shadows from nightly fires could be drawn,
Where spectral visions from primitive rituals were spawned.
Shadows from moonlight were cut like silhouettes upon the ground.
The munificent flame did rise and crown
Those souls that were never found.
When the torrent of its fervor was aroused
The serpent's fire bore no ire
Merely present with ritual and desire.
And the flood of its energy opened heaven's gate -
A pristine vision did quake -
Tube blown manganese and ochre fired those walls
Lit by rock lamps and burning animal fat that begat
The eternal light for them to see
A divination that sparked the golden light
That emanates like a beam -
With the clarity of a mountain stream but more than a dream-
And cradled in the skull until death,
Refined for drink- part of their scheme.
I had no skull to drink from
Cave drawings to prod me on
A gift it was – until it was gone.

Spirit of Blood

Roster of the Dead

Pictures of the dead
Impassively displayed
Those virginal faces
on a front-page spread.
lives that won't unfold -
Truncated stories that won't be told,
Their lineage forever on hold -
Cut short by a sniper's bullet –
A Delphic omen that was foretold?
Of a riddled body left on a road?
Perhaps it was shrapnel from an IED -
A weapon of dread that left many dead.
Two thousand according to the spread
A nice even number – those placid faces of the dead -
Their smiling portraits – no hint of their horror and dread
Or the heartless-way they were slain.
Their youth spent in vain -
Besot by heroism
And a quixotic stoicism.

Not all is lost
When their remains are tossed
In an urn or a grave to reside with the frost.
Their names are etched on a plaque
Or carved on a tomb with a knack.
There is no slack
When it comes to the dead
a number is granted so living can't be misled -
Pinned to their stripes for posterity -
Shows where they will be for all eternity.
It matters little what number they are -
If they are on the list - they are dead;
A youthful tableau reveals their dreadful end
As a maze of grieving loved ones
Shedding tears at graveyard venues –
their bond foregone - lost to a silent tenure.
Plaques in hometown places
Replace those youthful faces,
Alphabetically arranged by their names
Are all that remains
In rows like little death masks in black and white photos,

Peering through narrow windows.
Some are brazen - like an ancient bust of a roman;
Some are sullen as a Norseman.
A few have a baleful look of despair
With an unflinching commitment to their welfare.
Others look unshakeable and stoic
Itching, no doubt, to be heroic.
Their faces are buried in the shadows of time.
Residing in hometown shrines
Forgotten like so many raindrops sliding off a window pane.
Some never complained
When they were returned to the frozen tundra
Of Minnesota or North Dakota.
Some reside in the Iowa grass lands;
Others in the frost-free Texas rangelands;
The hardiest - in the bitter Wyoming flatlands.
A few preferred the humid tropical Everglades,
Where hurricanes have torrential tirades.
Some are buried in places with refined names –
Westminster, Dublin, or Exeter.
Others in well-known places like Chicago, New York, San Antonio.
A few are buried in places with poetic names like Pearl or Durango.
Lots of Whites, Woods, Smiths, and Taylors top the list of Anglos.
Some like Tilton, McClain, or Weigle look Oriental
Or Vasquez and look Occidental -
Mixed blood – not incidental.

Not all the dead are stateside born- Jaysine from Guam,
Tripped an IED - not much left to send home.
Some soldiers bear their progenitor's seed,
Inherit, without regret or shame, their father's name –
Jerry Reed II or William Wilson III - how germane -
Ordained by God or fate the seed of the next heir
Clipped their lineage – what despair.
Wives and daughters were on that list with fate's assist:
Tara Brown was shot down in Kabul;
Linda Pier got the same on her first tour to Gamberi
Lieutenant White was killed on site by an IED in Kandahar;
A road side bomb did the same to Erica Alecksen -
A Georgia girl, just twenty-one.
She perished in an instant – no time to be gallant.
Death had no preference who was chosen – gender mattered not -
Any soldier can be shot

Or shredded by whirling shrapnel from a hand grenade.
What are sons and daughters of the roster worth
After their mothers gave birth? -
Thrust harshly from their wombs into early tombs;
Their emblems and metals turned quickly to heirlooms.
What is left besides the press? -
After the obituaries and the photos are posted commemorating the dead? -
A hearse with wings brought them home
To a lowly tomb
A hometown dirge to a preacher's tune
After they are discarded in an earthly womb.
Their stoic gaze amid sympathy and praise
Is all that remains before a silent grave.
One red rose and a token flag to twist and wrench in sorrow and pain.
A burial site or an urn is due -
Ashes on a mantel have a comforting virtue –
The dead are always in view,
But remain a sad clue we can't undue.
A grave may be better to pursue,
Especially those buried long ago -
When the tears ended with an enduring furlough.

Lost Souls

The nameless dead,
Forgotten by God and man
A speck in time and nothing more
Lost in plague or a casualty of war
Neither memory or tombstone was a reward -
An anonymity under the sky
Nothing left to identify.
A burial by nature's hand perhaps:
A blizzard or a windswept storm or an avalanche
Left to atone and die alone.
A lonely man lost in the desert gasps his last breath
and perishes in the sun's rays – a painful death,
blanched and parched on this desecrated land
his bones scattered and buried by wind and sand.
The peasant perishes by a virulent plague
His corpse is tossed on a pyre - a life so vague.
His ashes - mingling with dust and wood
are swept away by a summer breeze- nothing understood,
unnamed and forgotten for all eternity.
The galley slave lost to a turbulent wave or a battle wound,
Without a plea
his flesh and bones washed clean by the sea,
a salty grave, cold and deep, deprived of stake or tomb -
Not even a memory is left to commemorate the gloom
Of their uncharted deaths.
those unclaimed myriads lost to the stars,
their munificence buried in unmarked graves -
lost even to time and memory without a single rave,
unseeded in the minds of men - tossed to oblivion's edge
like the still born infant abandoned in a prairie grave -
remembered by chance in poet's stray line
who felt bemused by their lives - left behind
in their silent retreat without an earthly glance
heard by him - their tortuous voices in a heartfelt trance,
lost by chance –
entirely misbegotten -
not even a memory that was forgotten.
An insufferable riddle, an enigma unsolved
that some souls suffer such a fate – unresolved,
and wincing when he knows
their lives were foreclosed.

nothing can be done to reclaim their past
nor is there breath to ask
how to bare a life that was never brought to bare
those quiet and desperate whispers of despair
Only the wind could share.
He dared to bare the lives of those parted few
that no one knew -
heralded the trumpet to awaken these dead
and their forgotten dread
within the minds of men,
and replenish the seeds of memory once again,
and let the muse bequeath a song to the living blood of the dead.
they let him know, in a single glance, life was cruel to a select few,
from his dark cavern he does hear a songbird in a meadow singing clear
that they once were by calling forth the muse to serve the dead.

Vietnam

The Augean burden that had no end
By invaders unbidden
Who left burned out huts and dead children -
And desecrated forests with a torrent
Using a Rainbow Herbicide defoliant
Without warrant
Where seeds are banned –
Can no longer claim the barren land.

The war of lost souls
With their terror-stricken dreams
Exploited, overused, rigged to go to battle by false claims,
Cheered on by misguided patriotism,
Returned to their homeland crippled and blind,
Sent to unwelcomed shores to die in a field or billet
From a sniper's bullet,
Or an IED - crude and instant
Cheap and easy to assemble -
An Everyman' s weapon,
An easy lesson
Will destroy a caisson
Fertilizer or TNT and a few wires and a fuse
Is all that is used
To leave many mangled corpses behind
On forlorn and dusty roads
Or packed away in body bags
Their names etched on lonely headstones.
Left alone
Except on holidays - is there a groan
Otherwise, forgotten and left alone
To pass the seasons with their bloodstone -
All they possess after their rest.

Some did cheer when they returned
Even the brave son who was spurned
By death's hand,
And skipped the ride home in a body bag.
Even amputees hobbling about after an IED
Ripped off a limb or a hand
Weren't denied their rightful pride
When they couldn't stand or shake a hand.
They sat in stands and cheered them on
Praising their bravery in Vietnam –
Those empty decrees and stinging palms - what a con.

The flags wave for those hollow men –
Their stolen lives for a senseless omen
Left to grind out their days without a spokesman
Drugs consoled them after they were broken.

The flag waved in effortless, unthinking patriotism,
Yellow ribbons stuck to SUVs like dandelions on fields of death,
Stiff and rigid, unyielding in a summer breeze -
Pinned emblems of our arrogance and callous loyalty.
"Support our troops" pasted on car bumpers
A rhetorical mockery of compassion, ad nauseam,
Mundane as a small-town parade.
Mediocrity kills and mediocrity makes murder and bloodshed noble -
Morality stripped of integrity,
A shell of itself, born of pretense
Based on pretext.
Burned out huts
And useless ruts
In the "land of a million bombs"
To punish their scions
Two hundred million cluster bombs -
Seven for every Laotian.
Those T-28 Trojans were a popular choice -
Many did rejoice
When the dead were announced.
More rejoiced
When the "Daisy Cutter"
Made more suffer.

Even an Augean war has to come to an end
When the losers subtend
And each declare a win.
Yet fail to see
In their glee
Death holds the garland after the brutal spree.

Propaganda was the underpin
More lives must be lost so the dead are sacrificed
Keep killing so those who died aren't undermined
Killing - feigned for glory's sake.

The Mantel

Discordant voices fill the air
"Persevere!"
"End the war!"
Mingle in the streets of despair
As flag draped caskets linger in hangers
Far from their gravesites and war time endeavors.
Awaiting their journey back to their home
Greeted by the bereaved - they aren't alone.
Red ribbons on porch posts gripping death.
Grave yards fill as onlookers kneel with an anxious breath
In the crepuscular maze of crosses length to breathe,
Resting supine in the misty fog
Dropped in a hole fresh from a synagogue
Or a chapel after the minister's monologue.
Some are novice to the grave;
Others are ancient to their enclave.
Neither can be missed -
On a mantel stands the portrait of a son
With a prideful smile that can't be dismissed -
Forever missed
As he poses in his cock-breasted uniform
Worn when he was undone.
Propped up by a cardboard flap –
A feeble wing to hold him steady and upright
For all to see – a vigil day or night.
Departed not long after he took leave of her loins
Pointing to the golden frame,
She enjoins that's my son in uniform -
A little coffin that bears her hero -
A keepsake of perennial sorrow -
A fallen warrior proud and sullen
Resting on a mantel.

Hollow Dreams

Rulers with hollow dreams
Stick together by any means -
Sovereigns of the aristocracy
Who send men on a fateful odyssey -
Make us proud they convincingly profess
After many deaths.
They devise a plan that inflates
And appeals to that delusional fate -
Kill those that support a communist state –
Adhere to these empty platitudes and inane creeds,
And be eager to return to the killing fields -
Don't question this cunning rhetoric -
Thought it best to question naught.
Truth unsought, they plowed forward and fought.
Propaganda and platitudes did reap,
Their staggering aim – and few did weep
as blood seeped on foreign soil so deep,
And life seemed so cheap,
And time showed no merit or a hopeful leap,
And the price of death became too steep,
As insurgents fill the streets.
What's at stake when mourners wait,
As coffins with embalmed remains
Are shipped home and nothings gained.
Others are mutilated and decomposed -
Burnt, bloated or crawling with maggots –
Never to hear propaganda from zealots.
Some are Identified with birth marks or tattoos –
Enough to sing their praises,
And feel their loved ones woos.
Those in pieces are mixed and matched -
A torso here and a hand there -none can be attached.
Those with missing tags are lost forever
Loved ones are left with painful displeasure -
Often kenning a mistaken successor.
Empty platitudes kept being pursued.
As those guns kept being renewed
As votes and money were never skewed.
Those body bags returned with little gratitude -
As those their plans never went askew,
A fabrication that caught hold -

Machiavelli would deem so bold -
An enviable deceit no one could defeat,
A first-rate design of a perfect kind -
Easily inclined that had to finally decline!

The carnage began to lose its mystique
The holy grail of patriotic blood became too bleak
the glory of death could no longer be a crutch
as the grand plan was now out of touch.
earnest pleas subdued those sophists' decrees.
The scheme soon became an afterthought -
The oppressed, blind to the hollow plight,
Ceased going along with the plot -
Master and slave had cohabitated in this device
One greatly gained the other paid the price.
They had failed to see through fog of deceit.
The few that protested were accused of a liberal ruse,
labels were used to defuse their views.
the standard "commies" and "anarchists" were used,
attempting to set their lofty goals aside -
forcing them to lose their stride;
Their lofty protests were construed as a crime -
especially those that were sublime
that undermined their misguided plans
that let the bane of poverty run rife upon the land -
and sent those to die and take the deadly stand,
preyed upon their disposition -
Indoctrinated them to their deviant inclinations
And they sacrificed their lives and destiny
At great cost and penalty.
While they died in the trenches
With unquestioning support without pretenses.
They played their nefarious game without the slightest shame,
Put the blame on those that complained.
Their enterprise to their pleasant surprise
gave them votes to avoid a compromise
overzealous patriotism simplified the rebellious candor,
allowed them to set the scale without a standard,
grabbing the weakest branch on reason's bough
to support their vows,
of their contrived plan
ignoring those who could not brook this wayward stand
and began to count those body bags.

So, off they went to Vietnam,
Conscripted men sent to war,
jungle shrubbery on their caps,
help prevent them from getting trapped
Acapulco gold steadied their nerves and made them bold -
Whatever cruel or heartless fate might unfold.
go out high in jungle and grass -
Dried mouth deaths were the best.
If they survived a skirmish or two
Another toke renewed their valor and their candor too,
Until fusillade of bullets or a grenade
Put an end to a heroic escapade.
They continued the jungle foray
Burning huts and villages
Watching peasants flee and die from this heartless pillage.

They forged on with a tireless war,
Devoid of an imminent rapport,
Dying in tangled brushwood,
And dense broad leaf forests
On those hot and humid days of death -
purged from the underbrush –
shrapnel filled or sniper killed.
Homeward bound in gray or blue,
clean and pressed - presentable for the priest -
another number on the screen - a mortician's dream.
As flag-draped caskets with conscripted remains,
buried with formaldehyde and pot in their veins -
waylaid from those wasteful campaigns
of decimating fields with agent orange,
cremating men in sniper nests and underground bunkers -
ready-made crematoriums -
a gunner's sanctuary.
No longer on watch for their adversary.
Their shriveled bodies, black as coal-
Nothing left to extol -
"Crispy critters" they were called,
Snickered at in their demise in bemused delight-
Did little to aid the fight.
They tried their best to beat them down
With daily bombs on villages and towns,
But nothing worked to kill their will.
But the blood torn road had nothing to instill

And the dead went unfulfilled.
The jungle war failed to bring about a calm.
Platitudes no longer glossed over their shame -
Worn out rhetoric failed to renew their weary claim,
Or gloss over their reckless aim.
Or the unflinching need to repeat this uncivil blunder again.
Time can numb the senses with too much sin -
The perfect dream of hollow men,
To peddle the cause they want to render,
And slander the rebels who wanted to hinder
The brutal adventure,
Ignoring the endgame of their deeds,
Ignoring the consequences of their schemes
Caught In the web of death and destruction.

Modern Warfare

Smart bombs dropped from a silent sky
Pilotless planes with an accurate eye,
instant carnage,
an antiseptic target -
bloodless, painless - an imperturbable harvest.
A simple mushroom cloud,
Perdition on a screen – death without a sound.
No face to stare down
Emitting an agonizing moan
No gasping for air - left to die alone.
No corpses imbedded in mud
No bodies to dispose of -
An instant faceless death.
No time for dread -
No posthumous regret
Just smoldering cremated corpses instead.

Nothing left but weightless coffins
Filled with pulverized bones and wedding rings –
Mostly dust and little other offerings
Is packed off to lowly graves.
Nothing grim with these remains
No open coffin no need to cremate
Dissolution only God could rebate.
A plume masks their instant demise.
No metals of bravery to mesmerize.
No feats of battle to dramatize.
No one in those graveyards at sunrise
Nothing more than a vacuous prize –
Just a button and a target and worthless cries.
Cheers and applauds - nothing left to eulogize -
Nothing left to memorialize.
Just a mist and a smile -
A remote pilot pleased to see such guile.

Spirit of Blood

Two times they took aim
To mark their sight to slain
The youth pondering on the plain
When the bell was clamoring out their pain.
One was spared
When bullets whistled by
But death caught her eye
When a 30-06 hit Miller in the face
His jawed displaced -
Dead before he buckled at the waist.
Blood spurted from his mouth
And spewed across the pavement
Like a mountain stream.
She watched it gush
Her hand did touch
That pulse of life
Squandered like the rest
Fallen from a 30-06.
She saw the heartless strike
Emanating from a spurious strife
And a penultimate moan
As his blood turned cold as a corpse's bone.
It dried upon her hand
Later washed away - but memories stand
And the dead from the Blanket Hill command.
Their spirits lay not in heaven's fall
Nor in heaven's grace -
Nor what there is to blame and extol -
But in the remnants of the Spirit of Blood
In the rusty bullet laden sculpture -
Spared the lascivious eye of the vulture.
In the lonely lifeless plaques -
Asterisks of the attack.
In our memory of innocence destroyed.
In our memory of tyranny opposed.
Men do not change
Their crafted edicts
Their iron clad decrees
May hinder their crafty motives – a temporary reprieve -
Stall their misguided deeds.
Still, the minatory schemes of yesteryear

Vex the land with despair and thoughtless cheer -
Old seeds planted in a new garden persevered!
Nourished by propaganda and zealotry –
A fatal devilry -
For the Spirit of Blood.

Thirteen Second Divide

Some memories are so bold,
They can't be purged of the torment they hold -
Or be erased
When they are faced.
Spring brings love but not in seventy -
A campus massacre sparked uncertainty,
Unrest rocked the streets,
Vexation and regret stirred our hearts -
Unrelenting as heartbeat.
The fault line of our discontent
Had settled at Kent State -
The thirteen second divide -
Caused our views to collide
When sixty-rounds
Sent oozing blood to the ground.
Aghast and stunned,
Those M-1s were destined
To whirl those 30-06s unconstrained.

Winter had relinquished its icy grip;
The burly winds of Lake Erie had been given the slip.
A mellow day of May fourth
Held a promise of rapport -
A hopeful respite from the riots and turmoil -
Broken windows and a fiery building that had come before.
The war and a broken truce -
No reconciling with the truth.
Effigies of the unscrupulous – images - cruel and obtuse
And caskets – facsimile of the dead -
Paraded through the streets with dread,
The protests spread and so did the dead.
Shots rang out on that sunny day in May
When the Guard was ordered to Blanket Hill
With a mission to kill.
Up the knoll of death, they did go,
Equipped with canisters of tear gas and live amo.
Company A, lead the way
On that fateful day,
As Canterbury commanded with a lethal sway,
Bull horn in hand he made his first demand to make them pay –
Disperse and live another day;

The students heard, in dismay,
His besetting them to obey.
Defiant they stood,
As they should,
As they refused to say farewell,
And took their aim near the Victory Bell.
The students scattered as they could
As he bellowed again through the megaphone;
These behests put the protest to the test;
Determined as he was, to put an end to their quest.
Canisters from Army stockades
Were launched by the brigade -
Twisting, twirling and spewing noxious clouds
As they bounced on the ground,
Burning their lungs and stinging their eyes
And the world became polarized
As students scattered through the smoky field
Until they settled near Blanket Hill
Above the commons and the Liberty Bell.
The Guardsman followed them to the grassy knoll
And took their toll -
Settling once to no avail
Settling twice to open fire -
"load, lock and fire" did transpire.
And those M1s unloaded at a rapid rate –
On that infamous date.
March fourth was filled with rounds of 30-06 -
Sixty-seven golden-tipped bullets
Raced toward their targets
With military ardor.
One hit Jeffrey Miller in the face;
He died instantly in his place –
No last thoughts to meditate.
Recumbent on asphalt and stone,
Mary Vecchio in supplication bemoaned,
As blood oozed from his head,
She was the saintly supplicant of the dead
After Jeffery had a collision with a piece of lead.
Forever etched in our wretched memories -
The iconic image of shock and dismay -
Innocence lost and the conscience of nation on display.
Scheuer was next to die –
No one could deny;

A bullet penetrated her neck -
Her oozing blood could not be held in check.
Krause and Schroder had time to reflect
Before their demise -
Shot in the chest - they lasted until sunrise.
Dean survived the M1 shell that severed his spine -
Crippled - lifeless below his waistline -
Spent his life in a wheel chair forever confined.
Stray bullets found a few more to wound
In the melee on that fateful day -
Those bullets found their way -
A thirteen second delay
Before the massacre –
Left an eternal mark on the calendar.
Three shots per second –
That's all it took to have a woeful awakening.
The thirteen second divide
Opened a perennial wound,
Without a means to mend,
Exposing an Inharmonious and painful rift,
Neither heaven or earth could shift
On that early spring day in May.

Seed of Destiny

It's too bad she's dead
Stiff and cold like lead
Unfathomably silent
The worst silence of all-
The final silence-
Worse than autumn leaves in the fall.
Years of fear and dread were shed-
When she relinquished in dread
Her mortal coil with whiskey and drugs.
Short lived as it was her efforts weren't in vain
Poems have been written in her name.
She desired to die young
Too soon from her mother's womb,
But not before hers was laden with the seed of life
Ordained as she was to be a wife.
In her cold silent vigil, she'll never know
After many a snow of years that come and go
The seed she nourished in her womb-
A windowless room dark as her tomb.
A pulse near-by like a friendly spy- comforted it with every beat-
That little soul did feel the heat-
A muse in blood so he could sleep
Before the pen does make him weep.
Before he learned the world was bleak,
The little poet flourished in his fleshy turret
Barricaded from the world's brutal current:
Men in metal turrets flew the skies
Unlike the poet met After their demise-
Their pelted bodies washed away-
Miscarriages in the sky-
flushed from lifeless wombs
in rotating tombs-
Barbettes of death and doom.
Bombs dropped in orchard fields and city blocks,
Murdered and maimed myriads of God's flocks,
Buried them in rubble-graves of concrete and steel.
Cyanide ovens made their appeal with genocidal zeal.
Fumigating bath chambers with Zyklon-B
Naked bodies- soap in-hand-strewn on concrete floors like worthless scree
Greedy Eviscerations for gems and precious stones
Before the crematoria turned them to bones.

Distraught sirens screeched warnings of death in the dusty night air
As cities were leveled with precision and care.
The little poet calmly slept in his lair
Dreamed breathless dreams he had to foreswear
Rife with love and despair
Until he felt wayward womb thrust him breathless into the earthly air.
Seeds of flesh and seeds of thought
were joined in blood and spirit bound
Among the trees and a forest breeze
Where fire flies floated in a dreamy field-a perfect frieze.
The sun perched upon the horizon with a resplendent haze.
But time would teach him to weep in dismay
Darkling plains of strife and melee
Etched a course without remorse in history's fateful pathway.

The Final Word

The Epistle

Our mantels are filled
With pictures of the dead.
Flags are draped on coffins with dread,
Graveyards are full of flowers with pain and regret -
Yet, it's not enough to soothe our broken hearts,
Not enough to forget ,
Not enough to curb the threat
To a servile debt
To the specter of death
To the Spirit of Blood –
Lives lost without a shrug.

The smoke-filled streets
Without a reckoning after a blitz.
The mushroom cloud
With radioactive clout
Turned flesh into irradiated dust.
Those trenches filled with the dead,
Bones buried in the mud
After a blast of mustard gas in artillery shells -
A toxic mist the eyes and skin beheld
Blind and scared it rarely failed
That certain death when the lungs inhaled -
A cinch they would be assailed.
Bayonets are meant to pierce the flesh
And cleft the heart
Casting the soul into the dark.

As the sun rises,
The days have many guises
The nightly stars are radiant in the sky –
One grand emerald that will never die.
Our desires always comply -
Never with a golden eye,
But to go awry
With vengeance and lies
Until we espy
That few are spared
The Spirit of Blood.

The voices of contempt
Are the fire of torment
Death is the only commandment
Peace may be a temporary respite
Before another atonement
Before another bloody battlement
Liters the fields of corpses
Yet we stand remorseless
With only one manifesto
That must be bestowed
That can't be veiled –
The Spirit of blood will prevail.

When The Lights Go Out

When the lights go out,
Whatever is left of us
Will be cast into space
With dust, bones, in a comic haze -
Star dust in a blaze.
Nothing will be left,
Not even a hint of life.
The earth and its seasons,
The fallen leaves,
The winter snows,
The quick pace of a summer doe,
The sunset glow,
Since time immemorial long ago
Will perish in the void of a breathless life
Without passion or strife.
No memories will survive -
Just a nameless void – no one to despise
No one to hate
No one to love –
Just the lost whisper of life
Like the autumn leaf
That disappears - so brief -
On the first winter breeze.

The Final Word

We work in shadows
Darker than a moonless meadow.
No sunlight shines in our soul;
No praise we can behold;
No stars bare our name.
We aren't to blame -
Smitten by our claim,
And fearful of our shame,
Especially when we reap no fame.
We toil and sweat on our own,
Imprisoned alone.
We continue to labor in vain
When that sudden surge unrestrained,
Rushes through our veins
Spawning verses without refrain
Despite those incredulous voices filled with disdain.

We are like slaves in a field;
Our fate is sealed;
Bent over in pain our faces are concealed
Our backs are broken -
Mere tokens
Of our lost life
Filled with the pain of a soulful strife.
Desire burns in our soul
As those ashes of despair
Perish in the flame.

Threats don't scare us.
Centuries of distress
Never made us digress.
Our verses thrived;
Our souls spent –
Nothing to show for our discontent.
We are never heard,
But the flame is never disturbed.
Even though we are estranged,
In those shadows we seek the sublime.

www.ingramcontent.com/pod-product-compliance
Lightning Source LLC
Chambersburg PA
CBHW022100090426
42743CB00008B/669